CONFESSIONS of an EX HOT MESS

10 Steps to Beat Stress and Feel Your Best

L.K. Elliott

Suite 300 - 990 Fort St
Victoria, BC, Canada, V8V 3K2
www.friesenpress.com

First Edition — 2015

Photography by Paul Buceta and Vanessa Wennerstrom.

ISBN
978-1-4602-5825-5 (Hardcover)
978-1-4602-5826-2 (Paperback)
978-1-4602-5827-9 (eBook)

1. Self-Help, Stress Management

Distributed to the trade by The Ingram Book Company

Table of Contents

Introduction

I didn't realize how depressed I had become until I had it all.

The perfect fiancée, engagement ring, job, house: you name it. From the outside in, it appeared my life gave me no reason to ever had a bad day, and yet I couldn't seem to get through a day without crying about how terrible it seemed to be.

My emotions had taken over my life, and I always had one negative thing or another that I would obsess over, or some method of self-sabotage I was practising. I grew up with a single mother with four children, and for my entire life I had one goal: to be happily married for life. But for some reason the moment I got engaged, a switch flipped within me that increased my craziness. It was as if subconsciously I wanted to push my fiancée away and I wanted to be miserable and alone the rest of my life. It seemed the closer I got to my ultimate goal, the harder I tried to make it fail.

After all, doing anything for anyone but myself was a foreign concept to me as an adult. From the age of six I took care of my mother while she was in an abusive relationship to my stepfather. I then spent the rest of my childhood helping her parent my three younger siblings. By the time I graduated high school, I felt I deserved to be selfish and leave all the BS behind.

I had also picked up all kinds of dysfunctional behaviours from my unpredictable childhood. From a never-ending list of things to worry about, to a complete void of confidence, to a lack of common sense — shall I continue? I knew I had issues, I knew they had to change, and I was the only one stopping myself from making any improvements. While half my brain was on board with change, the other half wasn't willing to accommodate anyone, not even myself unfortunately.

I found myself on a non-stop Ferris wheel of shit and the only ticket off of it required me to somehow transform my mind, which was getting crazier by the minute. To say I was stumped is an understatement. I was a lost cause as far as I was concerned. And this sense of hopelessness only fuelled that evil little voice in my head that told me all along, "You don't deserve happiness anyway!"

My name is LK Elliott, and I am an Ex Hot Mess!

After years of therapy I decided to try a little DIY project and began reading self-help books. What I found was a genre of books that were helpful, but sleep-inducing. I wanted so badly to learn the lessons from these world class self-help gurus, but I would struggle trying to make it through their medical jargon and lengthy chapters. From there I moved onto self-help audio programs, because I couldn't fall asleep while driving and listening, could I? After years of gaining knowledge in the self-help field, and finding methods that worked magic for my life, I wanted to pay it forward and help others out of their own darkness. I wanted to spread my message of hope to anyone willing to listen.

I gained the greatest knowledge in this journey by applying different self-help methods into my own life and analyzing what worked best for me. We are all very different creatures with different backgrounds and experiences. It took a lot of trial and error to find the right balance in my life, and the avenues that best served my well-being. I encourage everyone who reads this book to never stop searching for more information. We must grow daily, and there are unlimited possibilities for ways to improve our lives. Whether my methods work wonders for your life or not, there is always more to learn and more you can incorporate to improve your life's circumstances.

Throughout this book I will explain how I transformed myself from a complete disaster to a peaceful more balanced person who, dare I say, actually ENJOYS her life. It wasn't easy and it wasn't fast, but I have found some of the best methods from tons of sources and I have compiled them in this book in hopes that it might help you get through whatever it is you're looking to conquer. And unlike most of the self-help books I have encountered, I like to think I considered your entertainment needs while writing my *Confessions of an Ex Hot Mess.* I want you to enjoy the transformational process, and enjoy reading this book as well. I want the lessons within these pages to sink in, and that simply can't happen if you're drooling on them! Everything happens for a reason, and perhaps all of my missteps and embarrassing moments can serve a purpose on an entertainment level to keep you engaged as we move through the *Ten Steps to Beat Stress and Feel Your Best*!

If you have any dissatisfaction in your life, you have to make the choice today to fix that. It may be a circumstance in your life that needs changing, but most commonly it's simply the way you are perceiving things in your life.

I believe there are simply no reasons to be unhappy. Sure, things may not be exactly as you want them, but even that is a choice in itself. Either do something about it, or change your perception!

We've all heard the saying "Glass half full, or half empty" right? Well let's fill up your glass and get less crazy together. Your life is awaiting you! You may have doubts, that's natural, but if I can make this transformation, you sure as hell can! Believe me.

I'm a big believer in fate and I feel there's a reason you're holding this book right now. Something has brought you to this perfect moment and it's your time to shine, baby!

If you're ready to start living a life of fulfillment, and want to wake up every day excited for the opportunities each day brings, turn the page and let's get started.

Ingredients For A Sh*t Storm

Ask any great chef and they'll tell you that they don't need a cookbook to get the taste they desire. Over the years they have learned what works and what doesn't work. They know what spice is nice, and which will destroy what they are trying to create.

Well you can consider me the Iron Chef of Sh*t Storms. Like a good chef, I know all the ingredients that were required to have created a hot mess like myself. Each and every person on this earth is unique, and we all have our own recipe for the situation that we are in today. I'm going to list some of my main ingredients in the following chapters and hopefully you can find a few that you can relate to.

Some of you may have simpler recipes than others, with possibly one or two ingredients that have left you with an undesirable taste in your mouth. Or you can be like me, who is more of a Jambalaya of Crazy with all kinds of ingredients mixed together in one big bowl.

Each chapter in this volume will explain the *Ten Steps to Beat Stress and Feel Your Best*, and will break down the different factors that can leave us feeling imbalanced, and once we have recognized these issues, we can get to work on getting them the hell out of our lives! I recommend reading through the whole book, even if you don't think a certain topic relates to you, and once you have completed the entire book you can go back over the chapters that inspired you.

Each chapter will be summarized with a "The Gist of It" section, and following that will be an action based "The Fix for It" section. There are also a few activities included that helped me make changes in my life, I highly suggest you complete them regardless of how uncomfortable they might make you feel! Feeling uncomfortable is the first step towards growth. If you require more writing space to complete your activity, feel free to continue it in a journal or notebook. I have faith in you, so be open and honest with yourself and let's see what we can get accomplished throughout this book.

Results will come when they are earned, and not a moment sooner. So if you're skipping the exercises and putting in a lack of effort, you cannot expect your results to be amazing. Remember, the only difference between ordinary and extraordinary is just a little *extra.* Put in that little extra every day, make each step count, and watch your life transform!

Okay, enough small talk, let's get to the good stuff!

Rewriting Childhood Drama

I'm starting here because this is the first opportunity for stress to negatively affect your life; I believe the root of 90% of my issues all developed during my childhood. Sound familiar? There were so many issues I had to work through that I never realized stemmed from the stress of childhood until I was into my 20s. It's kind of amazing to think of all the mental damage that can be created in such a vulnerable time in your life. Any deviation from an average, happy childhood can seed little misconceptions about who you are, and how you should react in certain situations.

My earliest memories bring me back to a childhood full of dysfunction. My house was my own little hell on Earth, I felt as though I had no protection from the pain in this world, and from early on I knew that a lot of responsibility would fall onto my shoulders. Not exactly the best environment to develop as a human being.

During the times I was supposed to be growing and developing basic skills I was busy protecting my mother and siblings from an abusive step-dad, and trying to protect myself from a world of hurt all around me.

I vividly recall consoling my Mom on the floor after a verbally abusive attack one day, and in that moment it was sheer instincts to take care of her. I also watched as my younger brother was physically abused in front of me, and I recall being paralysed with fear. I never forgave myself for allowing that to happen and to this day I have a difficult time reliving those painful memories. Any hardships I had to endure seemed insignificant compared to seeing my loved ones hurt. But after years of feeling such fear and pain, everyone has a point where they can't continue on the way things are going. I hit rock bottom in Grade 6.

I will never forget the day I finally snapped. It was as I was getting ready for school and my step-dad was scolding my Mom across the hall. I had a moment where my fear flipped gears and became rage, and my 'flight' mentality switched to 'fight.' I stopped what I was doing and started to stare at what was going on. I was firmly instructed to close the bathroom door by my stepfather. I fired back with, "Stop yelling at my Mom." This was the first time such bravery had ever been displayed in our house and was enough to push him over the edge, so he stormed over to me, pushed me into the bathroom, and slammed the door for me. What happened next was a release of years of mental abuse, fear, anger, and the need to protect my family.

When I opened that door I felt no fear whatsoever and I showed that by shouting every profanity I had ever heard in my short lifetime. I grabbed everything within my reach and began throwing them at him. I had had enough. If my Mom wasn't going to fix things, then I would. I screamed until I had nothing left to say, and threw everything until my arms gave out. I stormed out the front door without my shoes vowing to never walk foot in that door again. And I never did.

This was the first dysfunctional lesson I taught myself: fighting gets me whatever I want and need. And fear is not a viable option. I vowed to myself to never feel fearful or vulnerable again, I would always be the hunter and never the hunted. I'll get to how this would destroy any chance I had at a functional life, for years to come, later in this book.

After that outburst I headed to my father's house and explained I'd never go back. My mom was forced into submission and decided to leave my step-dad's house for good. I know she did it for me, because she would have stayed forever if I hadn't insisted otherwise. In fact, three years later she moved back to the same town as him to try and reconcile. That's the thing with abuse and dysfunction, it rots your soul but once you get a taste for it it's hard to have anything else.

Back to my biological father: it was right around this incident that he really began to participate in my life. Prior to Grade 6 he was absent and too busy partying and enjoying his life to be bothered with parental duties. I lost count how many times I was left disappointed when he was "too busy" for his kid's visitations, even though they were only every other weekend. And on the weekends he was able to fit us into his schedule, he would host huge house parties that went late into the night. While my beer fetching abilities were a huge party hit, it wasn't exactly the bonding time I needed as a child.

And for good measures let's add waking up to make beer can pyramids (quietly so not to wake my Dad of course) and meeting whoever his flavour of the weekend might be. There is nothing more horrid than waking your Dad up because you want to spend time with him, and realizing that wavy hair in his bed belonged to some random woman. I recall feeling my first bouts of depression at my Dad's house. That's not to say I didn't feel miserable at home with my step-dad but the direct abuse was distracting and kept my mind active. I felt an emptiness within and it was only during quiet times that I would really notice that dark cloud cast its shadows over me. Taking the time now to relate those feelings to adult depression, I can recognize how early in my life I became anxious and depressed.

Having an abusive stepfather and an absentee father left me with all kinds of self-confidence and abandonment issues. I spent most of my teenage years seeking love in other ways. I'll get back to that later as well; I assure you it is colourful. The issues were rooted deep inside of me, and it is something I am just now beginning to overcome.

Now to round off my roster of parents, I will have to reflect on my mother's methods of parenting. While she was able to express her love, and imprint that on us children, she was unable to get her own sh*t in order. She was naive from the moment she met my father, and her life became an unpredictable roller coaster after that. She liked to see the best in people, even if that person abused her and her children. She denies ever knowing about him abusing her children, but even after she was told, she still admitted that he was the one for her. Sighhhh. Moving on.

One of the worst feelings growing up was knowing that I had no protection. I had to protect my family and myself when in an abusive household, and I had to hold my own when my Mom was parenting us solo. I took on a lot and felt extremely responsible for my siblings. It wasn't until recently that I connected this responsibility to the masculine energy I had adopted, and practised regularly up until a few years ago. I couldn't handle feeling weak, so vulnerability and emotions were off the menu, indefinitely.

Besides my Mom picking out these two fabulous fathers for her children, she did try her best to provide us with what we needed. Unfortunately stability was one need she could not afford. We were constantly moving houses. A trailer, a townhouse, and for a blissful month, a camper in her friend's front yard. Being a single mom isn't easy and you've got to be creative, but this did make it hard for a preteen trying to plant some roots down anywhere.

That pretty much sums up my childhood. I may be leaving out squabbles between parents about custody, child support payments, and dirty socks. Divorce has a funny way of turning life into a battlefield. But for the most part my childhood wasn't terrible. My single-mom home was full of love, wherever we lived, and we never went without. But the damage was done for this child, having been robbed the simplicities that I needed to develop as a half-normal adult. Luckily, it seemed my younger siblings missed most of the drama, and that brought me peace to a degree.

Maybe my sob story is peanuts to yours. Maybe mine sounds horrid. The stories aren't what's important, it's the effects they created in our development as little human beings that count. Take a moment to think about a few things that may have changed or challenged your development. The sooner we tackle these terrible things we don't want to think about, the sooner we can be free of them. There will be a section to write these events down in the next portion of the chapter.

Children are sponges and they absorb so much in those critical years of childhood, so when they are forced to grow up too quickly, they tend to learn a lot about things they shouldn't know about, and miss out on developing simple coping skills and other general abilities we need to succeed in life.

The issue is that being the resilient creatures that we are, we can normally push a lot of our issues to the furthest point of our subconscious minds, to deal with at another time. As kids, life is pretty simple: go to school, do your homework, play with friends. So even in an unideal home, you can survive and thrive in the darkest of situations. It's when 'real life' begins that things get a little sticky.

College, relationships, bills, car payments, etc. It's when these real life stresses mix with those back burner issues you've been harbouring for years that life goes to hell in a hand basket. I didn't even realize the issues I had until I was living alone in a big city far from home. I'd wake up having panic attacks about things that happened when I was 7. *Whoa;* not cool. I thought those memories were forgotten a long time ago, why were they haunting me now?

The truth is, they never left me. And now my body was *too* full of stress (old and new) and it was busting at the seams. But I continued the art of ignorance, and kept pushing my problems away. I'd fill that empty void with booze and boys.

Alcohol had a way of erasing my confidence issues for a short time, and attracting boys helped with my abandonment issues. Unfortunately, both left me with hangovers and my insecurities more damaged than when I started. In the moment, I was too busy seeking refuge to realize what I was doing.

If hockey-playing boys were treating me terribly, then maybe I'd hang out with the lacrosse team. Yeah, that'll fix this void in my heart — dramatic pause — but it didn't! I participated in a non-stop Easter egg hunt for happiness, and I was sure once I found someone who truly loved me that I would find happiness. That must be the key!

The day came when I had a beautiful house, a fiancée who love me unconditionally, a great job, nice car. The works. You must th

I would be happy then right? Absolutely not. I was still miserable — imagine that disappointment. I had everything I'd ever wanted and was still not happy. How incredibly unfair.

My childhood drama taught me all about dysfunction and survival, but never gave me time to learn about coping with daily stress, having healthy relationships, and living with trust. So no matter how great things were in that moment, there was always a thorn in my side that enraged me, someone who could leave me and something that could go wrong in the future. I couldn't be in the moment because I was so damaged by the past and fearful of the future.

I constantly focused on the minuscule negatives in my life, even if they plagued me only 1% of the time. I would dedicate almost all of my efforts to that one thing. To an outsider it must sound ludicrous, but it was the way I had lived my entire life. My childhood was full of fears and worries, so I continued on with that mentality into my 20s, despite the circumstances in my life being very different. It was the only way I knew how to live.

One of the hardest things I had to do was recognize that I wasn't living the same life as I had when I was a child. I no longer had to worry about eviction, abuse, or money. Everything was under control and nothing negative that existed in my childhood was present anymore, but the habits that were created in surviving my childhood were still running daily. I was always worried, but in reality my worries were empty. I was always afraid, but in reality I had nothing to fear. Recognizing this simple fact helped me break these habits.

Once I consciously discovered that I was living with the same fearful mentality as my childish self, I had to do some work with my subconscious mind to mend the issues. Our subconscious mind is the part of our brain that works behind the scenes. It stores a lot of our history in its memory bank and creates a breeding ground for our inse-
-ities to multiply and hold us hostage. This is why we often overreact
-iately; often the incident itself isn't the cause for our reaction,
-s that have built up over time in our lives. Our over-
the compound effect of past hurts mixing with
-reate an overwhelming stress to our psyche.

Our reaction often comes out as anger, when in fact the true emotions we feel are hurt, disappointment, and sadness.

I find visualization is a very effective way to work with our subconscious mind to clear out old clutter from our past. Imagine cleaning out the closets of our minds, and throwing away the old habits, fears, and pain that no longer serve us. Something I found to be very effective is taking the time to visualize myself at a very young and vulnerable age (I picked my grade 3 self, at the height of my fright) and have a conversation with yourself in a happy, safe place. We must understand that these old habits are not meant to inconvenience us, but rather to protect us from pain. When we were young, we developed habits and mental patterns as a way to survive, so our subconscious mind believes that those behaviours are required our entire lives to survive. It is only when we can communicate clearly with ourselves (and our subconscious mind) that we can finally alter the way we are behaving and feeling about life.

I laid down in my bed, closed my eyes, and envisioned my sweet little grade 3 self sitting on a bench. I sat down beside my younger self and thanked her for being so strong for all these years. "Thank you for protecting me, and for helping me get to where I am today," I praised her. "I need you to understand that I'm all grown up now, and I can take care of myself from now on." If you are getting the impression I have lost my mind at this point, I can't say I blame you, but I also need you to understand how incredibly therapeutic this experience was for me. Tears were shed, and burdens were left behind forever after having this internal conversation. There was a part of my subconscious that refused to let go, and this conversation helped explain why I needed to let go, and that I would be alright in the future without the overwhelming stress that I continued to participate in daily as an attempt to avoid pain.

I continued explaining why my life was very different now, and that I now had a great support system around me to lean on if times ever got tough again. Verbalizing these facts internally really helped me move on and accept the life I was living in, and gave me a new foundation in which to build my future on. It was my first step of many to begin creating a new outlook on life, and more confidence in my own abilities to react to life's stresses accordingly, as they occurred.

Take a moment now to give it a try if you'd like. I found it very intimidating at first, and it brought me a lot of sadness to think about myself at such a vulnerable age, and all that this little child was going through. But we cannot move forward if we are continually looking backwards, and by cutting these ties once and for all, our attention will remain where it should be focused: on our wonderful future. This experience was a very emotional moment for me, but I let the emotions flow. It was a part of the release. Purging these past hurts is vital to feeling better, and the discomfort you feel in these moments only make you stronger.

Becoming comfortable reflecting on your childhood is the first step in this journey, because how can we destroy a monster we cannot see? Each painful memory you relive is simply putting a face on an obstacle you must overcome.

Self-examination is the key to insight, which is the key to wisdom
- M. Scott-Peck

The Gist of It

The most difficult and productive way to move past these past hurts is to recognize them in the first place. Maybe you're like me, and kept the memories locked up deep inside you. Let them loose. Maybe you don't really know what the issue is.. Take some time to think about your past and how certain things may have affected you.

This doesn't have to be when you were a child. You could have been a teenager, or you could have been in your twenties. Perhaps you've waited until you are in your fifties to change your life. Life doesn't stop at a particular age, and experiences can change your life at any time, so think about an event or person that changed your life in some way along the way.

I've listed below my own personal circumstances, and how they affected me in my adulthood. Maybe yours are similar, and maybe not. But take a minute to think about things that happened in your past (childhood, adulthood, whenever) that may have changed who you are today. Maybe you had an awesome childhood, so you could put some positives down that affected your life for the better. The important thing is to reflect, and then we'll get to the Fix!

Here are a few of my examples:

The Action	*The Effect*
Not protecting abused brother	Self-hate, insecurity
Mentally abusive step-father	Insecurity, anger as protection
No protection from parents	Insecurity, anger as protection
Absentee Father	Insecurities, abandonment issues, hunger for acceptance
Gr 6 Melt Down/Move Out	Proved my temper can accomplish anything, positive reinforcement

Please take some time now to write down a few of your own life experiences that you feel have impacted your life, for better or worse. Think of what action or event occurred, and the effect it had on you emotionally. Making these connections is the first step in creating a change in the patterns these effects have created.

The Action	*The Effect*
______________________________	______________________________
______________________________	______________________________
______________________________	______________________________
______________________________	______________________________
______________________________	______________________________
______________________________	______________________________

The Fix For It

Here is the best part. No matter what happened to you as a child, it does not have to affect you negatively today. That is a fact. Disappointment is simply a by-product of an expectation not being met. So if you take the time and actions to change your perspective, and drop your expectations of what your past *should* have been, you can free yourself of these unhealthy feelings.

I realize this sounds too simple to be true, but I promise you it is. I have studied a lot about cognitive therapy; for those of you who are not familiar, cognitive therapy is a psychotherapy that states you can change the way you feel, by changing the way you think. It's an unbelievable topic that I will go into more detail further in this book.

An important fact of cognitive therapy is that with practice, you can reprogram your mind to see situations differently. You can look into the past with an entirely different outlook, and look into the future with a wonderful new perspective. But it takes work and practice. Nothing this beneficial can come easy. But let's try an example.

One of the greatest things I ever did to change my perspective of my childhood or any past event or relationship, was to rewrite it.

Take a second, and think about it. Rewrite your own history. There's always a positive or negative spin on any story you tell, and I guarantee you can turn your terrible childhood into a much improved one. For example, a woman changed her perception of her multiple adoptions as a child from a sad childhood full of rejection to an excellent opportunity to meet so many great families.

You may be raising your eyebrow and thinking this is ridiculous. But let me tell you, the second I put pen to paper I was able to turn every sad or troublesome event into a happy one. I puked rainbows all over my childhood, and it felt so good.

Creating this new history of yours will be similar to building a new highway exit to your past. Before rewriting your past, you would look back at your childhood through sad eyes, and that was the only exit your mind knew to take, to get to your childhood. That mental exit must be shut down. I'm talking ROAD CLOSED signs, and maybe blow up the bridge if need be.

Once you've written down your new and improved childhood, it's going to seem fake and strange. When you think of your childhood you'll naturally go to take your old exit that you've taken your whole life. But you'll see the bridge was blown up and will eventually remember the new exit to take. It'll seem like a pain at first, because you're used to taking the old route. It may feel inconvenient and unnatural at first, but give it time. Eventually you'll forget about the old exit, and whenever you think of your childhood, you'll naturally take the happy exit. This is an example of subliminal programming, and it truly works.

Again, if it sounds like I'm taking crazy pills, I probably am. But I'm happy, so you better buck up and take some too! Just try it. What's the worst thing that can happen? You've spent 5 minutes of your time. I have gone to therapy for years trying to get over this childhood baggage, and this was a defining moment in my childhood change of heart. My new story reads clearly in my mind and it has erased a lot of subconscious stress I had been carrying around with me my whole life. Through rewriting my past and keeping more fond memories of my childhood, I have found it easier to begin forgiving those who hurt me in my early stages of life. It truly has changed my life, because prior to this exercise I carried around a sadness subconsciously about my childhood, and that is now gone. I can now reflect on the good in my childhood, and appreciate that while my childhood may not have been perfect, it certainly could have been worse. I survived, I have a great life today, and I know how to love with all my heart. So why be sad about things that happened 20 years ago? I'd much rather spend my time enjoying this moment, this day, and this life that I have built for myself.

Now it's your turn: think of a specific situation in your past that brings you pain to think about, and then try to think of all the positives you can pull from those situations. For example, I wrote that in my childhood I learned so much about life by having a more independent upbringing, and my relationships with my siblings were much stronger growing up due to the hardships we experienced together. And I certainly appreciate the wonderful love in my life today, which seems extraordinary in contrast to my childhood. I also recognized that all three of my parents did the absolute best that they could with the skills and experience that they had, which was extremely important to understand. Quite often we will label ourselves victims, without acknowledging that our parents often had issues of their own, including childhood drama. Once we take the time to understand that they truly did parent us to the best of their ability, while balancing their own battles internally, we can begin to forgive for past offences. This exercise was my first step in forgiving, and moving forward without carrying the burden of my childhood pain. Give it a try below:

Rewrite your history with positivity and love (pick a few specific experiences to start with, then feel free to write your whole childhood if you'd like. The more you rewrite, the better you will feel):

____

____

____

____

____

____

____

____

____

Now I'm not claiming this new story is going to cure all of your pains, but I do believe that if your issues began during your childhood, that this is a great first step. We'll work on resentments, fears, and whatever else you're battling with in upcoming chapters.

The most important thing I want you to take from this chapter is that remembering sad memories or reliving past hurts is the key to creating inner peace regarding your past. If you continue to ignore and avoid your past, it will always haunt you. Changing this pattern is painful at first, but it gets better. By not only identifying each and every letdown, but rewriting them, you can truly take away the pain in those old memories, and you can celebrate the positives that you were able to pull from them. I have rewritten many experiences from my past, and every now and then a new one will resurface. Rather than analyzing how terrible it felt, I go right back to this exercise and rewrite it with a more positive spin. There is always a silver lining in every story, no matter how grim it may seem. The difficult thing is letting go and allowing yourself to find that silver lining, there is no shame in wanting to live your life with positivity.

It is time to live your life without all that unnecessary suffering. Let's move on to the next task at hand.

Releasing Resentments

Resentment is something that comes so naturally to many of us, and we believe it is serving us in some way. Little do we know resentment rarely affects the person we are resenting, but brings negativity into our own lives unnecessarily. It is a terrible habit, and one that we must conquer once and for all in order to enjoy our lives completely.

Resentment was something I cherished and put a lot of effort into. I liked to think I had two variations of my resentment:

1. Resentment for past offences that hadn't been duplicated in years.

2. Resentments that happened, and continued to happen.

I was a pretty angry individual internally for most of my life, and although I wasn't always aware of it, it leaked into everything that I did. I thrived on drama. I could beat anyone in an argument, and was extremely confrontational. Winning pissing contests is where I attempted to increase my bankrupt confidence bank.

If I didn't like someone, everyone would know, and I would build my own resentment into a public affair. That drama fuelled me, and made me feel important. So with a chip constantly on my shoulder, I graduated and moved away to start my new life. As soon as high school ended I realized that resentment didn't work as effectively as it used to. Significance was harder to earn the more mature you were expected to be.

I like to compare my mental stress capacity to a dinner plate. Most people have moderate amounts of stress in their life, like a nice balanced meal. The food represents different stresses that occur in our lives, past and present. But my passion for revenge and grudge holding added more and more food to my plate, to the point where a traffic jam would send me into a panic attack because my plate was *way* too full already. You see, there was no space for the little stresses in life because I opted to keep my dinner plate at max capacity at all times. I had no coping skills, and no room for the crap that life insists on testing you with on a daily basis.

Despite my logical self seeing how futile this behaviour was, it was a skill I developed at a young age and I hadn't realized how much anger I had harboured until I began my transformation. I had a lot of people on my shit list and I wasn't exactly sure how I would get over it. It was my way of life. It made me feel alive. In the past, I had always carried around my resentments like badges of honour, but it was such a heavy load to haul around all day the older I got.

Resentment is like drinking poison and expecting the other person to die
-Nelson Mandela

ad reasons to be angry or resentful, I realized it was
harm. If I forgave them it would not be accepting
r, but it would be releasing me from these chains

that I had shackled myself in. And so I went on a forgiveness spree where almost everyone was off the hook. At first it felt like I might have been giving up in a battle of sorts, but what is more important in your life: to be right or to be happy? I picked the latter, and it has been doing me wonders.

So that took care of my pesky 'old school' resentments, but what do I do about the people that are still currently doing me wrong? And that's when it hit me: We speak the same language!

So rather than harbour frustrations, and allow my resentment to build unstably high like a game of Jenga, I could have a conversation with them. It seems so simple, and that's what I'm finding with my own self-improvement. The steps are simple, but you have to experience raw emotions and let go of things, and I think that is what people get hung up on and want to avoid. We must begin to look at results when we feel like avoiding short-term pain because otherwise we will miss every opportunity to make things better.

Speaking with people about your feelings puts you in a vulnerable position, and that is uncomfortable for many people, myself included. But by confronting issues head on and being proactive rather than reactive, you can cut a lot of stress out of your life. Obvious stress, and some more subtle versions too.

Humans try to avoid pain at all costs, and we create fears regarding situations to avoid the potential of being hurt in the future. We feel fear of failure and fear of rejection, but we rarely confront the fact that our misery will never go away unless we resolve these issues. Most fears never come true, but leaving a volatile situation in the same state will guarantee you will continue feeling your current pain. Rather than fearing far-fetched potential outcomes, acknowledge that things will never improve if you do not take risks and conquer these low-grade fears. It's a classic example of short-term pain for long-term gain!

Step one of dealing with confrontation is to try to remember that if these people have any staying power in your life, they will probably be understanding to your sensitivities and what you need from them. I find the more often I honestly express my feelings successfully, and they are received without resistance, the more confident I am in expressing them the next time. It's the old "practise makes perfect" deal. Start with one resentment at a time. Tick them off a list one by one, and once you've got a few down on your belt you will become more confident in the process. It's never going to be easy, but seeing a successful pattern will at least convince you that the short term discomfort will be worth the end result.

I have had a troubled relationship with my father for as long as I've known him, and half the problem was that I accepted the relationship as-is, without realizing it could be any different. He is a good man, but one who was never held accountable for his behaviour (not unlike myself up until recently), and thus continued on with his life unaware of the negative impact he had on others. This was one of the hardest decisions I've ever made in my life. Having deep rooted 'daddy issues' meant I was desperate for a relationship with him, which is why I accepted it for the dysfunctional mess that it was, but I had to risk it all, and put my foot down to achieve the relationship I had always truly hoped for.

I sent him an e-mail saying our relationship was inappropriate, and I wanted to basically change everything. To say he was blind-sided was an understatement, and we debated back and forth until I got my point across. I didn't speak with him for about a year and wouldn't accept any relationship with him until he vowed to change. I had no idea what the outcome would be, but that was something I had accepted before I sent my initial message. It was a very powerless situation, as the final decisions really ended up in my dad's court. He respected my request for distance, and that time apart really help me analyze how I was feeling. But around that year mark, he fully accepted what I said. He vowed to change, and admitted that failure was never an option for our relationship. This gave me a glimmer of hope I hadn't seen in my lifetime: that I might have a healthy father-daughter relationship after all.

We met up once shortly after that conversation (we live far away from one another) and I was shocked at the transformation he had made. He was appropriate, respectful, and genuine. I couldn't have dreamt of a better outcome. On top of his transformation, he also thanked me because I had delivered a message he had never received before, and it changed his life for the better. He is now in a serious relationship, and life has never been better. And I have a father I'm so proud of, and a stronger relationship than we ever would have had without that intervention. It built my own confidence for many reasons: Dad was willing to do so much for our relationship (my broken inner child was elated), I was brave enough to take that stand for my own well-being, and that I was able to create a positive outcome for myself after 25+ years of discomfort.

When we feel resentment towards a person there is always the potential for healing because we can always confront the person who we feel is wronging us. But what about external situations that exist or discrimination we feel on a larger level? Things like racism, sexism, and poverty. These are external battles that are very real for a large portion of the population, and these barriers can truly impact the quality of people's lives. But how can we move on from circumstances that are still occurring on a daily basis, and that we cannot confront directly? I believe you must look yourself in the mirror and begin assessing your self-worth to start with. You must convince yourself of your worth, and know wholeheartedly that other people's opinions or treatment of you is not a reflection of you as a person, but rather a reflection of themselves. You cannot control anyone but yourself in this life, and that means that you ultimately have the choice in whether you would like your life's struggles to define you and keep you down, or would you like them to fuel you to be the very best version of you that you can be.

Putting your energy and focus into the things that are lacking in your life, will only ever bring more of that lack. But if you can release yourself of this resentment, and begin focusing your attention on the things that you are grateful for, you will begin to bring more of that into your life. The fix for any hardship in your life is love; it is always love. You need enough self-love to know that you are worthy of all good things, and you need to know that what other people think about you has no impact on who you are as a person. There are thousands of people in this world who have met you, and they all have different opinions of you. If you let another person's impression of you define you, then you're going to be in for a world of hurt. The only opinion that matters is your own opinion of you, and that can be changed if it is not favourable at the moment. We will discuss self-love much more in the next chapter, '*Repairing Relationships.*'

It doesn't take long searching online to find an inspiring story of someone who came from nothing, and accomplished their wildest dreams. I just watched a movie on the first African-American baseball player to ever play in the Major Leagues, and his story was heartbreaking. He endured more pain and abuse than most, and simply used that as a daily reminder of why he insisted on being such a success. He worked harder despite the hardships. And if you can find a way to take your pain and use it for productivity and growth, then what in this world can stop you from accomplishing your dreams?

Resentment can consume a lot of your focus and attention, where it could be invested in something much more productive. So rather than dwelling on the fact that certain external circumstances are not ideal, try and think of ways in which you can make the current circumstances work for you. Know in your heart that you are exactly where you are supposed to be, and that everything in life (good and bad) is occurring to teach you valuable lessons about life. They are happening to make you a stronger person. So do not allow your suffering to be in vain; take the lessons that life gives you and grow bigger and better each day that passes, despite how hard it may be at times.

Find an inspirational story that moves you and read it every single day, and when the going gets tough for you think of how that person would have acted in your situation. Remember that for as long as there has been success, there have been struggles. The people you read about in history as extraordinary successes have simply found a way to endure and defy the struggles that elude them during their journey. Decide today that you will not allow another day to go to waste thinking about how unfair life is. Let go of your past, forgive those who wrong you, and stay focused on your own success story.

How boring would your success story be if there were no hardships? Sometimes I like to think of my life as an autobiography, and when things get hard I think, "Well this is going to make a fantastic chapter in my book!" Whatever helps you laugh through the moments when you want to cry, that is where strength is built. It is all a choice. It is all *your* choice. Defy the pain, and keep moving forward.

The Gist Of It

The moral of the story is: Resentment doesn't accomplish anything, and is nothing more than a waste of energy. It will never fix a situation, or even improve one. It will eat away at you and will subconsciously burden your life in the slightest of ways, but when you have truly dealt with a resentment, and laid it down for good, you can feel the weight lift from your shoulders, and you wonder how you ever carried it around for so long.

There is no easy way out of many issues. There must be confrontation. There must be a solution. You must prepare for the worst, but hope for the best and just have faith that whatever is meant to be, will be. My dad could have given up and I could have lost him forever. And if that was the case, that probably would have been for the best, but I can now see the importance of weeding out the negativity. And in many cases, that means specific people in general.

Albert Einstein defined insanity as "doing the same thing repeatedly and expecting different results," so how do you expect a situation to change without doing something differently? Conquer the initial fear and voice your concerns. *Create* the relationships you desire by holding yourself, and those in your life, accountable for what they are bringing into your life.

If certain toxic influences in your life refuse to change, then it's up to you to change and move on. Negative people are like tornados: they show up, bring chaos into your life, and when they are gone you are left to pick up the pieces. You wouldn't be friends with a tornado right? So why in the hell do these people belong in your friends circle?

Imagine heat is positivity and these negative people are ice cubes in your soup. It's going to be a lot harder keeping that soup warm with a bunch of ice cubes in it correct? Screw the ice cubes! Accept the fact that this person doesn't care about you as much as you always wished they would and move on. That one substantial hurt will be less damaging than a lifetime of constant disappointment and heartbreak, I promise you. It's like a Band-Aid you've become attached to. Just rip that sucker off and the skin will grow back. Out of sight, out of mind. I didn't invent that saying, but it's the truth!

If you are struggling with an external source of pain, from barriers that are out of your control, choose to forgive and choose to succeed despite the circumstances at hand. We are all born into very different situations, some easier than others, but we also all have potential within that cannot be taken from us by discrimination. The only person with the power to stop us is ourselves. If someone says something to us, we decide to allow those words hurt our feelings. The best way to combat discrimination is with love. Love your enemies, because they are in a much worst place than you are. Never allow yourself to feel like the victim, and never allow yourself to believe that bullies are better than you. They are much weaker than you, and that is why they feel the need to attack you. If they were not intimidated or threatened by you in any way, why would they invest their energy in trying to hurt you? It wouldn't make sense, would it?

Taking the high road is not always easy, but I have never met a person who ever regretted taking that path. It allows us to grow stronger and with a better sense of self-worth. We do not need to stoop to other people's levels, if they have an issue with you then they are investing their own time unwisely. And while they are wasting their own time trying to deter you from success, you'll be investing your time in work to be a better person, and achieving things that they will never be able to match.

The only disadvantages in life are the ones that we perceive to be true. Being an underdog has always worked in my favour. There are limited expectations and it gives you the freedom to exceed everyone's perceptions of what you're capable of! You must simply choose to invest your time and energy into your own potential, rather than in resentment and discouragement for your current situation.

The Fix For It

Set the boundaries and expectations that you need to be happy, and don't compromise. People are meant to fit into your life and if they don't, it's got to mean something. You're going to be a nervous wreck before these confrontations, and you're going to fear the worst, but just know that you are taking a brave step for your well-being, and that in the end you will be better off for it. Regardless of the outcome.

Step two is finding the method of communication that works best for you. In a perfect world, you would have a face-to-face conversation and all will be fine. But for me personally, I communicate best through writing (as you may have guessed since you're reading my book) and that is the method that I most frequently use. I find I can get my point across more clearly, and my message is undistracted by replies and questions. Some may think it's cowardly, but it works for me. I also appreciate having the opportunity to edit my words before sending them, which is not possible when I'm talking a mile a minute.

So if you need to speak, write, or send smoke signals to your bothered beloved ones to get your needs met, and then get that fire burning! Just get it off your chest already, and the healing can begin from that point on.

The initial confrontation is like the old military trick of setting fire to gunpowder in a bad wound. It will hurt like hell at first, but it will also seal your wound, and allow it to begin healing. Leaving a wound open is only ever going to allow it to get worse. Let's also be reminded that we aren't in the trenches, so we can take the time to clean out all the debris first. Ensure the wound is perfectly prepared to be sealed, and then close it as a clean, fresh wound ready to heal.

So recognize and clean the wound, seal that sucker up, and let the healing commence. It's that simple.

For resentments with a single person, communication will always be your best method of confronting the issues. But for those external, general barriers that cannot be confronted so simply, we must choose to value our self-worth and invest our time on growth and gratitude rather than resentments. It's a choice that is not always easy to make, but what alternative do you have? Will you invest all of your time fighting society for its injustices and discrimination? Would it not be a better use of your valuable time to fight for your own right to be a successful, happy individual who is indifferent to the behaviour of others? Trying to control others is a battle you will never win, because the only person you can control is yourself. So stop doubting yourself, resenting others, and accepting barriers that others have placed on you and start doing something to better yourself. This is your moment to shine, and be sure to beam a light so bright that even your critics cannot deny your level of success.

This is a war for your well-being, so basic bravery and communication will be required. The confidence in knowing that you deserve healthy relationships and a happier life today will be your ultimate weapon! So let me hear your battle cry!

Repairing Relationships

Relationships are complicated — with other people and especially with ourselves. But when we apply positive techniques in our day-to-day lives, that positivity will spread to all other aspects of our lives, including those delicate relationships that we cherish so much!

Let's start with our relationships with ourselves, because without a solid sense of self-love you'll never be where you need to be with anyone else. Every relationship will suffer to some degree without finding self-acceptance and treating yourself like your own best friend.

To get an idea of where we stand today, let's think about things we do to ourselves that we would never consider doing to our best friends. If your best friend gained a bit of weight during the holidays would you mention it? What about something to the tune of "Holy crap you're getting fat!" or "This is disgusting"? But.. Have you ever thought that to yourself while gazing in the mirror? No? Me neither (rolling eyes).

What about if your best friend said something kind of odd in the office, would you tell her to "Shut up, you sound like a moron?" And yet, have you ever said that internally to yourself? "I can't believe you would say something so stupid!" What about that one?

The fact of the matter is, we are *way* harder on ourselves than we would ever be on anyone else, ever! We have anywhere from 12,000 to 60,000 thoughts over the span of a day, and startlingly enough up to 80% of those are negative thoughts. Unfortunately many of those negative thoughts are directed at us internally in form of self-talk. Self-talk is one of the greatest tools we have for change, but it can also be the most damaging if we are not taking control of the messages we are sending ourselves.[1]

As many as 98% of our thoughts are the exact same every single day, so if we have a habit of thinking the same negative thoughts about ourselves, we will drill it into our minds daily, until we are completely convinced of it. So if we made the choice to turn it all around and be our own biggest cheerleaders, and really made a habit of that, could you imagine the impact it would have on our progress? It's unbelievable to really consider the potential that change could create.

We must begin accepting ourselves completely in each moment and showing ourselves love every day in the way we communicate to ourselves. That means developing a best friend relationship with yourself. Think of any bad breakup you've had in the past; ultimately there was something about that person that you couldn't accept, and so you were deemed incompatible. Well I hate to break the news to you, but if there are things about yourself you find unacceptable, you don't have the option of dumping yourself.

Since can't leave yourself, I'd say you have two clear choices for action: change the things you don't like, or accept them fully and unconditionally. Now the action plan for each item is entirely up to you, but I recommend you take some time and write these things down. There are so many things we can be insecure about internally, but it's important to analyze these insecurities and figure out which ones actually need to be changed, and which ones you need to learn to love!

First, we need to set the BS aside and just own our quirks. Know that each and every element of ourselves is what makes us unique, and that there are people in our lives who love these little things that we hate about ourselves. Unless you have a thirst for blood or something, and then I'm not sure anyone really appreciates that. But assuming you're not a vampire, you are most likely an amazing person who brings a lot to the table. All of the people around you see it, and yet *you* don't see it. Can you see how unfortunate that is?

Now in reading this, I'm kind of in shock myself. I'm having a moment where I've seen how far I have come in my own journey, and it's pretty awesome. I have always been that 'larger than life' type of person, you know, the one that everyone can hear at any group function. I came across as confident as can be, but I was really paralysed by a fear that people didn't like me. I had a weird way of showing it, I realize that now.

But the fact of the matter was, until I could find it in my heart to love myself, I would never feel confident that anyone else could ever truly love me either. And that fear caused me to build giant walls around myself, so that I could allow people to get close to me, but not *too* close. Not close enough that I could get hurt, even though subconsciously I was hurting myself by eliminating any chance for real connection to the people around me. They were connected to some facade of myself, one that I felt was most suitable to the situation.

I pursued things like playing hockey, Canada's favourite sport, to feel significant and that filled my void for self-acceptance. I could chalk up the teams I played for, and the level in which I got to compete and see tangible results to feel proud of. But not once did I feel *I* was exceptional, only my achievements were. I found my own self-satisfaction in pleasing others. I would strive to be the best in every sport I competed in and that was a point of pride for me, because it pleased others and made others think highly of me. This had nothing to do with my own self-reflection. This wasn't something I recognized until recently.

I literally had no idea who I was as a person up until the past year, because I had spent a lifetime trying to be someone I thought people would like. I'd tell jokes so people thought I was funny, I'd play sports so they'd admire that I was athletic, I'd even throw in some chewing tobacco if it would impress my guy friends in the moment (because I was *so* hard-core). But at the end of the day, I liked to be more sensitive and quiet. I really enjoyed giggling with friends, and having no pressure to entertain them. There was a very small group of people who saw this vulnerable side of me, and those were the times in my life I cherished the most.

Entertaining people can do wonders if you are insecure about yourself, because people take a general interest in you. But because you act so differently than your most natural state it only pulls you further from self-acceptance, because what they are accepting is not necessarily you. That thought scared the hell out of me, because I felt like people came to expect a certain demeanour from me, and I feared they might be disappointed if I was more subdued. And while I'll admit that many people questioned if I was feeling okay the first few times I tried to go out in public without being the attention seeker I've always been, they all eventually accepted it. And now I feel freer to do what I want to do and have lost that pressure to always be the life of the party. Now I attract people into my life who are like-minded, and who like the fact that I'm not totally ridiculous. Let's throw a disclaimer out there that I will always be somewhat outrageous, but at least now I'm being authentic! And I know that people are taking an interest in me, not a version of myself I've created to be more interesting: just me.

So if we can do some self-exploration and figure out who we truly are, and take a bold step to accept ourselves with open arms, regardless of what we would like to change; that would be a lovely first few steps. Now I need you to look in the mirror, and say out loud to yourself, "I accept myself fully in this moment." And mean it. At first you're going to feel like a crazy person talking to yourself in the mirror, and you might even look away because you know you're full on lying to yourself, but bear with me! Say it again with more passion, more truth:

"I accept myself fully in this moment." There, doesn't that feel a little good? Just a little? Again, at first it will seem as unnatural as hot pink zebras, but it'll feel more and more natural as you practice.

We need to speak out loud to our subconscious and let ourselves know that regardless of how we felt in the past, we completely love ourselves right now, as is. The more you can tell yourself "I love you" throughout your day, the better off you will be. At first it's going to seem weird, and you might even have little negative interruptions after you say it, but just dismiss it and repeat "I love you."

Mirror work is especially effective because when you look into your own eyes and say something meaningful, your eyes will reflect back to you exactly how you feel about that statement. I have had a good cry session after simply telling myself "I love you" in the mirror. It hurt because in the past I knew I didn't love myself, and it felt so good to hear in that moment. It was a strange combination of emotions, but it was powerful. It is something I avoided for a long time, because it takes extreme vulnerability and is a very raw moment that you must share with yourself, but the more often you do it, the more comfortable it becomes. Mirror work can answer all kinds of questions, you just need to build the courage to ask yourself!

In order to create the habit of self-love, you absolutely *must* reinforce it all day, every day until you start to feel change from within. We repeat our exact thoughts 98% of the time, so if we are used to repeating negative mantras to ourselves, we need to replace them all with positive ones! This will take some time to adjust to. I repeat the affirmations "I love you" and "I accept you" as many times as possible throughout the day. I say these affirmations out loud or internally at least 300-500 times every single day, and it has become one of my greatest tools in establishing self-love. The more you say it, the more you begin to believe it. You can say it to yourself when you are pleased with yourself, and especially when you're feeling disappointed in yourself or your actions. Self-love has been one of those tough things for me to train my mind into after so many years of not loving myself, but I am now feeling better than I ever have about myself and I truly believe it is because I have adopted this simple habit.

Accept the mistakes you made in the past, because they all taught you lessons. Accept your body for what it is today, because it's the only one you've got (and you can make drastic changes any time you want to). Be proud of yourself for every good thing you do in a day. If you can't celebrate your little victories, who can? You need to pick up some pom poms and cheer yourself to victory!

Again this probably sounds too simple to be true, but honestly almost *all* of our life's problems are a simple flip of a switch internally when we make the decision to live with positivity and passion!

Be supportive of yourself, just like you would your very best friend, and see where life takes you!

Once you've started to truly love yourself, for all of your flaws, unique qualities, and silly mistakes, you will notice that people become more drawn to you. You are like a magnet for love, and that is because like attracts like. You love yourself, you feel great, so you make others around you feel great. And they want to spend their lives with you in it. It's as easy as that.

So now that you have people noticing your awesome positive vibes, and they want to spend more time with you — how can you create meaningful relationships with them? Obviously this isn't your first time making a friend, so you understand the basics of how this works. But I have a few things I want you to be mindful of to make the most of your relationships.

Pain and pleasure have little to do with the circumstances in your life, but rather your own rules for what defines pain and pleasure to you. For example, if you asked three women whether they are happy with their bodies, they would all have very different definitions for what it would take to make them happy. For one woman it could be six pack abs, for another it could be to be able to run a marathon, for another it could simply be to weigh less than 200lbs. Can you see how different rules for each person create their pain or pleasure? Many people would be happy with the body I am currently building for my first ever bikini competition, but I know this is nowhere near where I need to be to be stage-ready. My rules are different to achieve a certain level of personal satisfaction with my body.

You have subconscious rules for every part of your life: your body, being successful, and definitely relationships.

Many of these rules were either created when we were young (and not quite so wise as we are today) or they were adopted from our parents. Think about it, we learned so much from our parents growing up (even if it was the perfect examples of what *not* to do) and we inherited many values and morals from them. Our rules can be changed at any point in time, but first we must define what they are.

We need to take the time to reflect and write down what our rules are for relationships. We can have rules that are unattainable to ourselves, or to our partners. We will go into specifics in the Fix For It section, but know that our unhappiness can be solely caused by our rules for how we think things should be. That thought or expectation can rob you of a happy and healthy relationship. You'll find in this chapter, and consequently in your life, that many things you were once unhappy with are more of a figment of your imagination than an actual problem. I'll give another example below.

In many situations in our lives, our reactions are based entirely on past experiences in similar situations. We recall past hurt and disappointments, and react based on how we felt in those moments of our past. How many times have you overreacted to someone and later found out that you interpreted the situation as much worse than it was in your own mind? Think of someone being a half hour late for a date, and you sit there and stew about how terrible of a person they are and wonder why you even let them talk you into dating them. You think about how this person obviously doesn't care about you, how selfish it is of them to leave you waiting, and you reflect on how rude they are too. Then you get the phone call explaining that they were in a car accident, and that they just hopped in a cab because their car has been towed, they feel terrible for keeping you waiting but will be there shortly. Damn, don't you feel like an asshole?

But prior to that phone call, while you were waiting on their arrival, you subconsciously reflected on every man, woman, or animal who has ever taken advantage of you and hurt your feelings. If you have ever been stood up for a date in the past, all of those painful memories were right there with you, as you marinated in the pain of past disappointments. Can you see how the past can affect your reactions today?

One of the greatest questions you can ever ask yourself before reacting to any situation is this: What else could this mean?

Could your reaction have to do with past resentments you've been carrying around about something completely different? Could you have communicated better to this person so that they 100% understood when you were meeting, and at what time? Could this reaction have nothing at all to do with this person, but perhaps your workplace is driving you a little crazy and you were simply blowing off steam? There are endless possibilities. And simply being mindful of them all will help avoid unnecessary issues in the future. Don't get me wrong, there will be days when people do things that are wrong and hurt you, and communication will need to take place, but it's sifting out the issues that aren't legitimate from the ones that are that is key. This works equally well for family, friends, and lovers.

We as humans are born with the basic need for loving connection, and it is an absolute requirement for our own survival. As infants we can fail to thrive if we are not physically shown love upon being born, and as we grow older (despite negative experiences in the past) we continue to yearn for this love. Why do you think that is? What is it about having a partner in life that makes life so rewarding?

Essentially, we are looking for someone to share our life experiences with. Plain and simple, we want to share our highs alongside someone, and we are looking for support during our hard times. Is there anything more comforting than having someone there when you really need them? To have a shoulder to cry on when it's required? The only thing better than a shoulder to cry on is to have someone to celebrate with you when things are going fantastic,to have someone to share your joy with when you get that dream job. It wouldn't be the same if you were home alone, now would it? No, not even ten cats will suffice in that situation!

If you truly feel that life is better or easier without an intimate relationship, there are clearly issues with your associations to intimacy. You have linked pain to the subject in your mind, and hopefully this book will help you find that connection to yourself, which will inevitably improve your relationships with others.But surely you can see the benefit to having strong friendships at least, right?

If we all unanimously agree that having friends (and maybe a partner too) are better than not, then why do we struggle so hard with keeping relationships healthy? Obviously friendships are much easier to sustain because the needs are usually less demanding than an intimate relationship, and there is less expectation and opportunity for issues.

I'm going to spend the majority of my time on intimate relationships, but friendships can unfortunately get a little sticky as well. I will briefly go over friendships and then move onto the juicy stuff.

At the end of the day, if you have a difficult friend who is always fighting with you, or stressing you out, it's time to let them go. I'm a firm believer in positive energy, and people bring one of two things into your life: positive or negative energy. It's very simple — one always outweighs the other, and if a certain friend is constantly bringing negative energy or situations into your life, they probably are hurting you more than helping you. Even if it's a 50/50 split, that's a lot of negativity you're receiving from that one relationship.

We've all had that friend, the one that is a walking disaster and who calls you at god awful times crying because they have made the same mistake for the 101st time.You love them, so you feel a sense of responsibility for them, and feel much too guilty to cut ties with them. I went on for years with multiple friendships that were volatile to my mental stability and well-being, but I couldn't find the courage to take a stand for my own happiness and health in stopping these negative experiences from happening.

That all changed when I decided to put my own needs at the top of my priority list. Ultimately, when we allow people to consistently negatively affect our lives, we are subconsciously choosing that they are more important than ourselves. Perhaps this is not the advice you expected from me, but it is the advice that I am giving. If you want mental balance, you must surround yourself with positivity. Life is hard enough without carrying the burdens of other people's life decisions along with you too. I'm not suggesting cut ties with any of your friends who has issues, because believe me, we *all* have issues. But there are people who refuse to help themselves, and will continue down the same path again and again, and they will drag you down that path with them. That is when you must take a stand, and explain your situation with them. You may feel responsible to take care of this person, but you must remember that you are a person too. When will you take care of yourself, and rid your life of this negativity, pain, and stress?

I know this struggle well, but followed through and had multiple conversations that went just like this: "I'm so sorry, but I am trying to make a major life change and I need nothing but positive influence right now, and the decisions you are making are really stressing me out, and distracting me from my own goals." Chances are these people will be upset and will think you're being ridiculous. This is because they see themselves as the highest priority over you, and this is your cue to do the same. Chances are in time, they will sort their stuff out and you'll reconnect again in the future, but by that time you'll be in a much stronger place emotionally, and hopefully they will be in a different place too. People will live up to the expectations that are set out for them, so if you expect the bare minimum, that is probably what they will deliver. If you state that you can only accept friends with positive behaviour and influence, you may be shocked at how people try harder to maintain that friendship.

You'll always care for that person, and make sure that they know this. Send them all of your love and well wishes but explain that you must love yourself first and foremost, and your own life path just isn't lining up with theirs anymore. You will always know which relationships you need to keep and which need to be cut. It's just whether or not you can be honest enough with yourself. It may seem mean or cruel to distance yourself from people who need you, but isn't is equally unfair and cruel to yourself to allow their negative presence to affect your life? Relationships must be give and take, and if you are the only one giving positivity you aren't doing yourself any favours. I feel your pain, I was there, but believe me — it gets better! And when everyone in your life is bringing nothing but light and positivity to you, you will be amazed at how life begins to shift, and you will wonder what you were ever doing carrying around other people's burdens.

So we've established a strong, loving relationship with ourselves and weeded out the negative people in our lives, and now we have met this great life partner. The first three months are the sweetest months of your life, you are so in love you can barely handle it. Your friends have never seen you like this before, and you think he or she is the one. As time passes and seasons change, so too does your relationship begin to change.

Things aren't as great as they used to be; they are actually a little difficult now. Real life stresses begin to creep into your relationship, maybe you've even moved in together and you're realizing (s)he's a total slob. You can't help but question, what happened to Prince Charming? And when did I become such a bitch?

Now if you are anything like me, you totally missed out on seeing any good relationships growing up. I had my grandparents, but I saw them so rarely that I never really had an idea of what a healthy relationship looked like regularly. This was a fact I just discovered. (*See, internal growth is a never-ending journey, and you will always be learning and developing as you go!*) I had negative feelings about my relationship, and communication in particular, because I had a confusing view on relationships that I developed when I was younger. I had to make relationship assumptions growing up, for lack of true knowledge gained from seeing healthy relationships around me.

Seeing my parents fight often, and then seeing their second marriages deteriorate respectively, I had the misconception that fighting equals dysfunctional relationships, and that any form of negative communication was fighting. So if my husband's feelings were hurt, and a discussion was required, I would interpret that as a fight, and I was extremely defensive and disappointed. This negative association caused itty bitty issues to seem much larger of an issue than they truly were. Likewise, a conversation that should have peaked at a 2-4 on an intensity scale, would blow up to 10 because I was so worked up that we had yet another issue in our relationship. See how my rules affected my relationship?

Subconsciously I was linking a lot of pain to any conversation that went deeper, negatively, than the weather. For years I couldn't see I was doing this, and once it was discovered I couldn't figure out a way to stop this behaviour. This is because my rule said "a healthy relationship never has issues!"

Until my rules changed, my behaviour would never change.

My mom explained that she had the opposite issue as me growing up and that her parents were so perfect together (enjoying over 50+ years of blissful marriage) that she grew up thinking marriage was effortless. By not seeing any of the difficulty or conflict in marriage, she assumed it was easy to keep one another happy, just as her parents did. Boy was she in for a surprise when it came down to her first marriage. And then her second. So most of us have skewed perceptions of how relationships work, whether we are naive or jaded by our past experiences. We must take the time to reflect on how our exposure to relationships have affected the rules we follow when it comes to intimate relationships. Most often, we are completely oblivious to the lessons we learned as children about relationships, and we must uncover those deep rooted lessons, because they almost always affect our behaviour today.

The biggest lesson I learned about relationships is that just like the relationships we need to nurture with ourselves with self-love, we must put just as much effort into our intimate relationships. Relationships are hard work and anyone who tells you different is lying. I assumed that finding the "right guy" was the hard part and then we would simply breeze through life after that. Boy was I in for a surprise!

Think about it, you are taking two individual people, with different pasts and personalities, and putting them in one home for the rest of their lives, how can that be easy? Sure you love each other, but there are so many lessons that must be learned in order for the two of you to be working effectively together. I know this struggle first hand, because when I met my future-husband I was already in a relationship for three and a half years. When I met him, I couldn't get him off my mind and it was love at first sight. Three weeks after meeting him, I left my boyfriend and moved in with this man I barely knew. (Can you say drama?) I know exactly how difficult it was to make this work, as most people would have gradually worked their way into this stage of their life.

We both have had challenging childhoods, so we had a lot of love to give each other, and we have grown and challenged each other every step of the way, together. He is my absolute soul mate, and I still get excited to spend time with him every single day. But how do we keep that fire alive? Work! Hard work!

In any relationship situation you must look for a good fit, which is someone who fits with your rules and values. Think of your life as a sports team: What do you need to make your team as strong as possible? My husband and I are both so similar in certain ways and then very different in others, and this maintains balance and rhythm in our lives. I know that his great fit into my life is a main contributor to our happiness, but there is so much more than that!

We began our relationship in the harshest of conditions, and had so much to learn about each other in a short period of time. This forced us to develop strong communication from early on. Honesty was a top priority from day 1, because we had so much going on, communicating about our feelings and fears was the only way to make the relationship work. And out of that desperation came a strength that we have maintained over the years. If honesty is not a priority, communication cannot thrive. Without communication, you will not have a successful relationship. This is a fact.

People have been telling us for years that the "puppy love" phase will end, but we are still waiting for that day. We have made it our mission to show people that you can maintain your excitement and love and that it doesn't have to end. Just like with anything in life: *If you're not growing — you're dying*. So if your relationship stops growing, it will begin to die. You must always work for the result of a happy and healthy relationship and when that is your focus, that is exactly what will happen in your relationship. It's not always easy, because compromise always comes with a price, but if you focus on the happiness of your partner, there is nothing you won't do!

I used to feel like our relationship would one day feel easy, and that after working on certain aspects of our relationship that the hard work would be done. How foolish I was in thinking that! I have always asked couples that were married over 30 years what the secret was (because I sure as heck didn't see it growing up) and I always get the same answer: You must *work hard*. And that's not a 'work hard for a few years and then it will be easy,' it's work hard every single day and your relationship will be successful. I believe that is where our divorce rate has come from. 50 years ago divorce was a non-option, so you had no choice but to work at your relationship to make it work. I'm not implying relationships were perfect back then either, but quitting wasn't an option, and that is something I admire and wish more people would adopt as a relationship practice.

People today get married thinking "If it doesn't work out we can always get a divorce," and that is so incredibly damaging to the potential success of that relationship. There cannot be a Plan B when it comes to marriage, you should think long and hard before you make that commitment and make damn sure that this partner will do for the long haul! In the past, divorce was the ultimate pain; people would judge you and it simply wasn't something that was acceptable. Now it is shocking to hear about successful marriages, and that is a sad reality that we must take responsibility for and begin to make changes today to correct.

A simple question you need to ask yourself for the sake of your current relationship is:

How are you loving your spouse, to your standard or theirs?

This question is so simple, and so complicated all at once. Take a minute to think (if you are currently in a relationship) if you are loving your spouse in the way *they* need to be loved, or are you loving them the way *you* need to be loved? The question is so incredibly valuable if you ask yourself with an open mind. For me, I had an overwhelming feeling of "I don't know *how* he even needs to be loved!?" Can you see a problem with this picture? I had spent three years of our relationship loving my spouse in the way that I needed to be loved, but with no idea of what he perceived as being loved.

Prime example of the differences between our ideas of love: I love and appreciate when my husband does things for me, such as making me lunch if I'm hungry or grabbing things for me so I don't need to get up off the couch. Anything that he is willing to do for me to simplify my life is so incredibly appreciated, so I had been doing these little gestures for him because I know how much I like to receive it. Well imagine my surprise when he explains that not only does he *not* enjoy me doing things for him, but he actually hates it. I was so lost in this revelation.

As it turns out, my husband is a go-getter by definition, and he enjoys the process of doing work. If he is hungry, he enjoys preparing his food and having a role to play in the entire process right up to eating it. He feels pride in doing things for himself, and it gives him a feeling of fulfillment in life. So when I was showing him how much I love him by doing things for him, I was essentially taking away his fulfillment. Wow. Talk about counter-productive.

And the worst part is, at first, I couldn't accept this. I was loving him, and he was not only not accepting it, but also telling me my love wasn't good enough. I felt offended. I was loving him perfectly according to my own rules, that much I knew, but he still wasn't happy. I felt we weren't compatible, and I became worried for our future. And meanwhile, he was incredibly dissatisfied because he had clearly explained that he needed something else to feel loved, and I was not accepting his request. Can you see how this could have turned into a very volatile relationship had changes not been made? There was a lot of resentment and misunderstanding during this phase of our relationship.

It wasn't until I heard the question, *How are you loving your spouse, to your standard or theirs?* that the connection was finally made. In an instant it all became clear why he felt unhappy in our relationship at times, because he desperately wanted to feel loved (just like I did) and was willing to love me the way I needed to, but I was not willing to return the favour. And the result was him never feeling truly loved. Sure, at times he would feel love, but not in the way that he so desperately needed for fulfillment.

Once I had realized the critical mistake I had made, my next goal was to find out what love meant to my partner. How am I going to make him feel loved if I have no idea what that means to him? Thankfully we both speak English, so figuring out his definition for love was as simple as striking up a conversation with him that night! The response was overwhelming, not only did he give me all the answers that I needed to help him feel loved, but he also felt my love through the action of asking him what he needed. A lot of women love to talk, but we lack the ability to listen. This was a great lesson in how asking questions and really absorbing what he was telling me could change a relationship forever.

The fact of the matter was that I loved this man with all my heart, but I was showing him in ways that he didn't fully understand. Love is like a language at times, and not everyone speaks the same one; but rather than judging each other for not speaking the same language, we can try to communicate this ever-important message to them in a way they can comprehend.

This communication and expression of love is where success is created. Understanding that we are not all the same, and fully accepting the challenges this may create, is where success is created. Your partner knowing without a doubt that he or she is loved unconditionally is of the utmost importance in your relationship, and so it is your responsibility to learn the ways in which they wish to receive that love.

These lessons are opportunities for growth and self-improvement within your relationship, and this is the hard work that is required on a daily basis in order to have a successful relationship long-term. The choice is entirely yours in whether you want to do what is best for yourself in a relationship, or will you choose to do what is best for both of you in a relationship?

I truly hope you choose the latter and enjoy the rest of your life with a loved one nearby to enhance your experience.

The Gist of It

The most important relationship you'll ever have is not with friends, family, or even your spouse, but rather with yourself. Without unconditional love and compassion for yourself you can never truly love another individual to your full potential. You can certainly try, but you will be continually burdened with issues that will wreak havoc on your love life in subtle and not-so-subtle ways. The only way to truly learn to love is by turning our focus inward and finding the things we love about ourselves.

This begins by becoming aware of your inner chatter, and making the conscious decision to only accept the positives. Even if you are like me, and have spent your entire life filling your mind space with negativity and fear, you can make the choice to change your ways. It's literally that simple to start. The follow through takes a little more time, as you must learn to dismiss those habitual thoughts and immediately reply to yourself with "I love everything about myself in this moment." Make that a habit, and watch change occur immediately. We must learn to love ourselves no matter what the circumstance, no matter how badly you want to stick your foot in your mouth, and no matter how disappointed you may be in your actions. It is in those times of need that we need support and love from ourselves the most.

By the age of three we already have an idea of who we are, based upon our upbringing. We will tend to treat ourselves exactly as we were treated at that vulnerable age too, so it is imperative that we recognize that fearful, timid little three year old is still within us. Only this time we are the responsible guardian caring for this little being, and we can undo all of the wrongs that occurred in our past by taking one course of action: caring and loving ourselves unconditionally. Our inner child is a most beautiful, vulnerable spirit within us and it needs protection and love, just as we did physically as children. So rather than becoming mad at ourselves when we have done something foolish, try consoling and loving yourself through that moment of disappointment and see how that feels. We all aspire to be good and when things don't go according to plan, or we make mistakes, it is so easy to punish ourselves for our performance, when what we should be doing is supporting ourselves to do better next time. We can accomplish this by learning whatever lesson is to come from this situation, and move confidently into our future knowing we will be more prepared when a similar situation occurs again. There is no need to dwell on the past, because it is long gone; all we have is this moment, so let's start living like it.

Every relationship we engage in has a group of associated rules attached to it, and these rules are what dictate whether or not we are pleased within the relationship. If your spouse has an affair with someone, that would probably upset you, correct? One of your rules in that case would be that they may not have extramarital affairs. Now this might seem ridiculous because that rule is obvious and is a rule for every relationship right? Well not necessarily; there are groups in this world where a man has multiple wives, and obviously to those women it is perfectly acceptable, and expected even, for him to have intimate relationships outside of their marriage. We can all debate until we are blue in the face on the ethics involved in those arrangements, but the fact remains: we all make our own rules and our rules dictate our happiness within our relationships. So the call to action is to identify what your rules are for yourself, your friendships, and your intimate relationships.

Be as obvious as you need to be until you get to the deeper rooted rules that you have. You may be surprised at what you find. I found that a rule I had for myself was that I was not allowed to make mistakes. Ever. Mistakes meant I was a failure and unlovable. So if my husband ever needed to talk to me about something I needed to work on in our relationship, I would overreact and hate myself for it. Then he began not telling me things, because he knew how hard I took it, and that would leave him unsatisfied in our relationship. See how one little rule can have quite the ripple effect?

Knowing these rules will give you an opportunity to work on rules that you need to rid from your life. It will also bring up the core values that are very important to you, and you can take that knowledge and use it to better understand the current state of your relationships. You can share this information with your friends, family, and spouse and let them know what is important to you. The beauty is this will give them an opportunity to think about their own rules, and share those with you. It's incredible what a little self-discovery and communication can accomplish. You'll seriously be amazed.

Having a clear idea of what your rules are will naturally make you become curious about other people's rules, which will make you a better friend and partner, and it will also help you identify where issues in your current relationships are coming from. When you know your rules, it is much easier to identify which rule was broken to result in this negative emotion. With that knowledge comes power, and the ability to be more effective in your relationships.

These rules include what love means to each individual person, because it is all too clear that we all have our own interpretation on what love truly is. Some people need that verbal validation for love, while others have no need for verbal, but will require constant physical validation. It is tremendously important to understand what the people in your life require to feel loved. After all, you do love them, so why not have them recognize it in ways that they can comprehend and feel? It will not only cause the people in your life to be happier and more accepting of your love, but they will be more willing to give you the love that you desire too. What you give, you get.

Your relationship transformations will all begin in the first starting block: realization and communication. The first half of that process requires you to sit down with yourself and be honest about the state of your relationships. I'd suggest tackling these one by one, beginning with yourself. Then branch out to the relationships closest to you, and the ones giving you the most grief. Once you have established your lists, it is an absolute must to communicate these findings with the people you have brainstormed on. How will change ever happen if they don't know how you feel? They will never know your needs unless you tell them.

Friendships must be looked at more in terms of 'team fit' and how fluidly they fit in to your life. If a friend is causing you pain much more than she is bringing you happiness, you need to reevaluate that friendship. If you are serious about personal growth and change, negativity is going to do nothing but impede your progress; that much I can promise you. I don't care how long this relationship has been going on, if it is volatile you have two options: You can communicate your needs and put the ball in her court, and if she truly does care for you she will respect your needs and try to change for the sake of your relationship. Or, if this is something you have already tried and she did not respond, you can put your big girl (or boy) panties on and walk. It doesn't have to be spiteful departure, but you must explain calmly that while you love this person dearly, you love yourself more, and your growth and progress is your top priority, so you cannot allow this negativity to interfere with your results any longer. Wish them the best in life, and say you'd love to hear from them if they are ever in a better state in their life. Their burdens cannot become your burdens. Life is hard enough without putting the weight of your friend's worlds on your shoulders too! Release that responsibility that you have taken for them, and release it into the universe to deal with. You cannot help people who do not want to help themselves. This may seem a little cut-throat, but the fact of the matter is, you have one life to live and

I personally made a rule years ago that I am not going to live a life of misery to accommodate other people in my life. That is a sacrifice I am simply not willing to make any longer. I did in the past, and it brought me a lot of pain: but today is a new day and my life can be as positive as I choose, because I have cut ties with sources of continuous negativity.

We are in a time and age where intimate relationships are failing all around us, and we are not always raised knowing the values of keeping a relationship healthy. Communication is the key to building and maintaining a strong relationship.

Communication is like the blood of a relationship, bringing the necessary oxygen to all the areas of the body of the relationship that needs the boost. Without blood, there would be no oxygen circulated, and eventually the areas of your relationship will become unhealthy, weak, and non-existent. Long before it gets to that point, become the *heart* in your relationship. Be the one who begins this flow of life into your relationship. Pump health and vitality back into your relationship and in time, your partner will begin to do the same, because they will see how great it feels. That positive, healthy relationship will become so appealing that both parties will do anything they can to maintain it's greatness, and that is the formula for a long-lasting relationship full of love.

Any successful team requires a bonding between the players involved. If you have two teammates who only want what is best for themselves personally, how are they ever going to succeed in a game? They will be running in separate directions rather than working together to achieve greatness. In order for things to flow smoothly, it is critical that you realize you are both on the same team. At times this involves putting your own personal needs aside, to accomplish the greater good for your relationship. Is it more important to be right or to be happy? Well which one is more important? I can't smack you through the pages of this book, so I am going to assume that you chose happiness. Ultimately that is the decision you must make on a daily basis within your intimate relationship: do you pick happiness and love, or whatever else your mind convinces is best for you? It is always that simple, and if you can remember that question and ask it constantly to yourself, it will become easier letting go of little things that have got you worked up.

Serving yourself is not acceptable in a relationship. The more cohesion between two people in a relationship the better. I secretly cringe a little when I hear a woman say "WE are pregnant. "(Umm no, he is a man, thus *you* are pregnant) but I must reluctantly agree there is some validity to this statement. The words 'I,' 'me,' and 'my' should all be replaced with 'us,' 'we,' and 'ours.' Always. Especially when you're taking the plunge to get married: you're sharing last names and everything else from that moment on. It is crucially important that you bond with your partner and begin to see things as a whole, and not separated between the two of you. That separation of personalities is what causes (gasp!) separations of couples. When you two make a commitment together for life, mean it. Make that man or woman as much a part of you, as *you* are a part of you. When that is your reality, there is no option for divorce. If you get a terrible infection in your lungs, you don't cut a lung out and move on with your life. You nurture that lung and bring it back to health, because it is a part of you. Likewise if there are problems in your relationship, you must bring the relationship back to health.

When you begin to see your husband or wife as an irreplaceable part of you, you will begin working harder in your relationship. Plan B shouldn't be divorce, rather it should be to repair what is damaged. I don't care what my husband does in the future; we made a pact, and there was no fine print in those vows. You made a commitment, and now you should have to live with it. If people thought this way going into marriage, I think they might choose a bit more wisely. I hate hearing that people had suspicions their marriage wasn't going to work before they got married. Why make things complicated?

If two people go into a relationship with a clear idea of the needs of their spouse, and an understanding that marriage is hard work, every single day; there will be no divorce. Nothing is ever broken beyond repair, that is a fact. Where there is a will there is a way, and any relationship can be salvaged. I know someone who was paralysed from the neck down competing in judo. He was told he would never be able to walk again. He laid there paralysed for a whole year, and one day he decided he wasn't going to accept his fate, and he was going to turn it all around. Today you would never know he had been paralysed, as he is walking around without an issue; I don't even notice a limp! So if someone can turn something that hopeless around, could you not try truly forgiving your partner, and enjoying a fresh start? Is it really that impossible to imagine?

A relationship is like a house: When a light bulb burns out,
you do not go and buy a new house — you **fix** *the light bulb!*

Okay, so your relationship may be on the rocks but you see now that nothing is ever truly hopeless. So let's get to work on how to fix these relationships, and build stronger ones in the future!

The Fix For It

A serious contributor to my unhappiness in past relationships was the fact that I didn't have a specific or realistic idea of what a successful relationship looked like. Growing up with dysfunctional relationships all around me, and then participating in my own, left me with no idea of what a healthy one looked like. So I made up a fantasy healthy relationship subconsciously and imagined what that would look like, but allow me to emphasize the word *fantasy*, because it was not a realistic expectation for real life. My thought that any argument, disagreement, or fight meant ultimate doom and gloom was very unhealthy and put additional pressure on me and my husband. It was in that moment that I recognized the issue was not the relationship, but rather my perception of our relationship and what it meant to me to have a healthy relationship. Now, obviously there are healthy and unhealthy fights. If you are hating each other and being cruel, that is never healthy for a relationship under any circumstance. But disagreements are bound to happen when you put two completely different people and all their baggage into a house and now their two lives are combined into one.

It's a major life adjustment, and compromises must be made. Unfortunately compromises mean people don't always get what they want, so there is resistance, and from resistance you create resentments, and eventually bigger issues. It's identifying these issues and communicating them before they grow into something too large to repair. So we must all accept the fact that issues are inevitable, and we must find peace with the idea of conflict. Having a conflict isn't important, it's how you resolve this conflict that matters. The more fluently you can communicate and resolve issues, the stronger your relationship will be. A smooth sea never made a skilled sailor and the same concept applies to a relationship. If you have a relationship where there is never tough times to work through together, there will never be an opportunity to gain strength within the relationship.

Accept the good with the bad, because it all happens for a reason, and will teach you something. Always.

Communication is such an incredibly important part of any relationship and yet many of us are very weak in this skill. Yours truly is certainly guilty of this. If I am happy, I have no problems expressing that to anyone: my husband, co-workers, heck I'll tell a stranger walking down the road. When it comes to negative messages to share, however, I'd prefer avoiding it and pretending it never happened. The issue with this is your resentment or hurt within will simmer and grow and will affect your subconscious in ways you'd never expect. Your built up resentment will come out in point form during a conflict and your partner will have no idea any of those twenty situations even happened. Don't pretend like this hasn't happened to you: you are simply asked about the power bill, and then you turn it into the Great Chore Debate, where you expose your resentments for garbage day, laundry day, and the fact that he never wakes up with the baby in the middle of the night. Whoa, he was just asking casually if you knew why the power bill was so expensive this month. Awkward!

Communication is like a pressure relief valve for your body. When a little pressure gets cooked up inside and needs to be released, you can gently turn the nozzle and release it slowly and gracefully until you feel better, by way of a productive conversation. But if you choose to ignore the warning signals and leave that pressure inside, it's going to grow and inevitably explode and make a mess, by way of an overreaction and possibly an argument.

I personally don't enjoy delivering these messages because I fear I will hurt my partner's feelings, ruin a perfectly good day, cause a commotion, or that he will have things he doesn't like about me that he now feels entitled to share. But guess what? You have to do it anyway! We must communicate the good and bad in order to keep a strong relationship, to change patterns that are disempowering, and to relieve internal stress and pressure. When I take the time to look back now, it was extremely rare that my husband ever reacted even a fraction as badly as I expected. I let fear that I created myself (through uneducated assumptions) steer my decision making when it came to communication. It will never be an enjoyable process, but it can become a bearable and productive one. It is so incredibly important to stay connected with our life partners, and the only way to do that is to communicate. Unless your spouse owns a magic crystal ball, in which case you will never need to develop these communication skills because he can read your mind. It'd be a little creepy, but I guess it'd save you a little discomfort in the short term!

One of the biggest hurdles with this communication deal is the inevitable dose of vulnerability it will require to execute. Many of us hot messes have a big issue with feeling vulnerable, and I have dedicated an entire chapter to it because I feel it is so important to become comfortable with. I am a big gym goer, and I always say, "Success depends on how comfortable you can become with discomfort." I believe the same is true for vulnerability, communication, and relationships. Sure bringing up your needs and wants to your partner is going to feel slightly uncomfortable, but the more you can accept and challenge this discomfort, the closer you can get to success, and the relationship of your dreams. That burn in the gym that tears muscles is no different than that agony you feel when you need to bring up something uncomfortable with your partner. It's learning to become comfortable with that, and see the end result before you begin. That will help make the pain a bearable price to pay for happiness, and get less caught up in the discomfort of the situation.

Communication is a perfect example of practise makes perfect. You must conquer your fears and have faith that your relationship will be strong enough to handle any adversity it faces. If your relationship is so rocky that one conversation about your needs is enough to send this person running for the hills, then maybe let him or her run. A relationship is about two people having their needs met, so that they can enhance their life experience together. A relationship is unhealthy if there is not a free flow of communication. So once you realize the importance of communication, express that to your partner and begin practising it together. Just like anything at first, it won't be easy or comfortable, but you will learn and grow together, and there is nothing more encouraging than that in a relationship.

I am extremely fortunate that my husband is a very open man, who actually helped me discover the importance of communication, and made me realize my own need for improvement in that department. But I realize that not all partners are going to feel comfortable, or even accepting of this communication concept. This is where the communication begins: explaining why you need this from them and how you will work with them in a way that helps them become more comfortable. Explain how important they are to you, and that you want this love to last a lifetime, but in order for that to happen, adjustments must be made and communication must be adopted. Give them a chance to fill your ear! Maybe once they get started they won't be able to stop. Us women especially like to talk and talk and talk, and never give the men in our lives the opportunity to get a word in. Maybe you open up the lines of honest communication by asking questions and *listening*.

Disclaimer: by 'listening' I don't mean coming up with a reply while they are talking, thinking about something entirely different, or coming up with an argument because you disagree with what they have just said. I mean genuinely listening to and caring for what they are expressing and sharing. Having that compassionate attention might be enough positive reinforcement to show them how enjoyable the process can be. For me at first, I associated communication with getting some form of shit handed to me, but once I was shown that I can actually use the same lines of communication to voice my own needs and feelings, it was a whole other ball game! Show your partner this light, and encourage them to participate, maybe if they see some incentive in it to help their own issues, they will be more open to experiment with it. If you attack them for everything they are telling you, then you shouldn't be surprised when they don't want to participate.

When you have a relationship where communication flows easily, you can custom-design the perfect relationship that satisfies both people involved. You will be in a position to ask them what they require to feel loved and you can ask them about their rules for happiness. When you have a list in front of you of all of the ingredients it takes to make your partner happy, it is as simple as following directions for a recipe. And the recipe is a successful relationship! How great is that?

You don't need to read their minds, or think of things yourself, all you need to do is ask. It can't get simpler than that.

From there you can have an exchange of ideas for what this great little relationship needs, you can both compromise to make sure everyone is getting what they need (rather than just want) and from there you both have a clear vision of what is required on your end to make this commitment work in the long haul. Communication is an absolute priority in any healthy relationship, second only to work. So get to that first step, and then follow through with all of your heart as though your relationship depends on it, because it does!

Once we have opened those lines of communication with our spouse, we should be able to express our concerns on a daily basis to allow less pressure and resentment in our subconscious mind. With this new-found freedom, we can take this lesson a step further, with a focus on internal communication. As I discussed at the beginning of this chapter, the relationship we have with ourselves is the absolute most important relationship we will ever have and maintain in our lifetime. When we have put in the time and effort into creating this self-love, we can begin to make it work for us in our external relationships. Two heads are better than one right?! Well having two thoughts within can cause the same benefit. Now I'm not talking about multiple personalities, but I am referring to your conscious and subconscious mind. That little voice that questions every decision you make subconsciously, and sometimes is out to lunch, but at other times actually brings up valuable points.

Think of any diet you've ever been on. You see a cupcake and your mind immediately says "Mmm. Get in my belly!" but then you hear this little voice within that says "Should you reeeally be eating that? What about that hour of cardio we did this morning? And you had a treat over the weekend already." We typically tend to resent that little voice because it has now ruined your cupcake scheme by making you feel guilty, and thus taking almost all of the pleasure out of its calorie-rich frosting. So you walk away from the dessert.

Well that little voice from within can help you avoid misguided decisions outside of your diet as well. It is one of the most powerful tools you will ever use in your life! Think of this: you're about to over-react and just before you open your mouth, to unleash the rudest thing that you have ever uttered (today at least), a little voice disrupts you and says:

"STOP! Do you think maybe you're overreacting? What else could this possibly mean? Slow down, and think about this for a minute."

So now what? We stop and think it through. Maybe we realize that we are actually upset about something not even related to this situation. Maybe this pause has given us the time to really prioritize our life, and we decide that this was a silly argument and that loving this person tonight is more important than fighting. Imagine the possibilities!

For how often we demonize our inner voice for influencing us, it is always our conscious mind who makes all of the decisions throughout a day, our inner voice simply brings forth an option. If we could use this to our advantage when we are actually hearing a great idea, we could really avoid some pain. Better yet, if we could rewire and train our subconscious mind to get in sync with our goals and wishes in life, it could be programmed to advise us in the most productive ways imaginable.

We could have our own little cheerleader on the sidelines for every decision we make, one that encourages us to make the best decisions to align with our goals and dreams, and steers us away from potential disasters. We have conversations with ourselves all day long, so this is simply utilizing these conversations to improve our relationship with ourselves. And training our mind to work with us, rather than against us. The healthier this relationship is between your conscious and subconscious minds, the better you can learn to trust this voice, which is in all reality, your intuition and instinct. This relationship all begins with self-love.

The first way to establish this pattern of self-love is by vowing to stick to a very simple rule:

I will never criticize myself, ever.

This was a very difficult task for me, especially with my old rule of "Thou shall not make mistakes, ever," but I stuck with it. If I did criticize myself, I'd quickly dismiss the thought, reassure how much I loved myself, and then repeat the affirmation "I accept myself completely in this moment." This would not only take my negative thought and turn it into a positive one, but it also reminded myself of my self-love and made me feel good about myself.

Self-love is not the easiest thing to adopt, because we have lived our entire lives feeling a certain way about ourselves; but just like any other habit, if you give it enough time, it will become second nature. Walking wasn't easy when you first learned, but look at you now! You could walk and text at the same time now, I bet. The same can be said for positive thoughts and self-love. It becomes second nature, and in time it flows freely through your mind, and now when a negative thought pops up, it sticks out like a sore thumb and is quickly dismissed.

Affirmations are going to be extremely useful for your introduction into self-love as well, because you must program your conscious *and* subconscious mind in order for the transformation to be complete. Affirmations are a way to program your subconscious mind into truly believing what you are telling it. It is a very powerful way to create change in your life, but only if you believe in it!

For those of you who are unfamiliar, affirmations are carefully formatted statements that should be repeated to one's self and written down frequently. For an affirmation to be effective, it needs to be present tense, positive, personal and specific. So if we want to program our subconscious mind into loving ourselves, we would repeat affirmations such as:

- I love myself just the way I am.
- I feel good about who I am.

- I release the need for self-criticism.
- I am wonderful and wise.
- All is well in my world.
- I am unique and special, a true one of a kind.
- I am a good person.

There are a million affirmations you could create to help you feel good about yourself. Feel free to include anything about your appearance, friends and family, job, car, pets, home, and anything else that pleases you. This is your time to think of all the good you want in your life, and then state out loud, internally, or in writing how you deserve it. You are an amazing person who deserves all the good and abundance this world has to offer. Imagine repeating that one to yourself all day, and how great that would make you feel!

Every thought you have about yourself you will begin to believe in time, so if you are currently throwing a lot of trash talk to yourself, you are going to feel like garbage internally, it only makes sense. But if you continually praise yourself with the most loving, kind, and wonderful thoughts, it will eventually catch on and you will believe those instead. Give it some time, because just like anything else that's new, it's going to feel a little odd at first, but the more comfortable you become, the deeper this subliminal message can spread internally. Eventually affirmations will begin to feel less strange, and then from there, you begin to believe it. And that is where the magic happens, folks.

Because when you start to believe your affirmations, life begins to open up. I believe that when you are willing to start investing in yourself, the universe will begin to invest in you. Your own personal worth is increased greatly with affirmations, it's like each affirmation is a deposit into a mental bank account, and your self-worth will continue to increase and increase in time. And eventually, when you have enough loving treasure deposited within, this bank will pour its excess love into all your relationships, starting with the most important ones. You will begin to love purely, in a way you never could before. You will have more of yourself to give, and more of yourself to love, which will result in more affirmations, which will continue to top up this bank account of yours. You will be prosperous in love, and there is no better outcome than that. Money is only ever money, but love: that can actually 'buy' happiness!

When you truly love yourself, people will notice. You will sparkle from within and you will have a profound need to share your love with others. This love sharing is the foundation for amazing relationships that will last you a lifetime. When you love yourself, you forgive yourself quickly for any indiscretions you may make over your lifetime, and this forgiveness will make you so much more effective in your relationships with others.

Learning to love and accept your splendour as well as your blunders is all a part of this process. Learn to laugh at yourself, and you will learn this unconditional love and acceptance for who you are. Making mistakes is what makes us human, and loveable. This is the lesson I needed to teach myself. I made the realization that I expected perfection from myself, and if I made mistakes it meant I was unlovable and unacceptable. So I began to think about what I expect from my spouse, family, and friends. Lo and behold, I discovered that I do not expect perfection from any of the people I loved, and in fact, when the people I loved made mistakes it was endearing. I found it made them more relatable, made me want to help them, and made me love them even more (because they were human). Once I made this realization, I began to treat myself differently, with the same love and acceptance that I showed everyone else in my life.

Can you think of any rules you have for yourself that are disempowering? And how do your rules for yourself compare to the people you love in your life? Let's try an exercise to demonstrate the double standards we keep for ourselves. Think of a few rules that you feel about yourself, and what it will mean if you do not stick to these rules. Once you have a few written down and considered, ask yourself if you have any rules like this for other people, whether they are realistic, and how you would feel if the people you loved broke these rules.

Rules for Yourself:

____

What would it mean about yourself, if you broke this rule?

____

Rules for Yourself:

____

What would it mean about yourself, if you broke this rule?

____

Rules for Yourself:

____

What would it mean about yourself, if you broke this rule?

____

Rules for Others:

____

How would you feel, if they broke this rule?

____

Rules for Others:

____

How would you feel, if they broke this rule?

____

Rules for Others:

____

How would you feel, if they broke this rule?

____

I hope you were able to find a couple disempowering expectations that you hold for yourself, that aren't nearly as terrible for other people to fall short on. As soon as you realize that you have these expectations, and that they are unhealthy and unrealistic you can begin to adjust your thought patterns and begin accepting yourself. Even when you (gasp!) make a mistake.

As soon as I stopped criticizing myself, and began accepting myself fully and unconditionally, I began to breeze through life with ease. When you begin accepting yourself entirely, you truly do begin to love yourself for who you are. And from there others can begin to love you too!

And while we are on the topics of rules, can you think of a few relationship rules you have? What are things you absolutely *must* have in a relationship to be happy, and what are things you absolutely *must not* have in order to be happy? Give the exercise below a try to get you thinking.

For me, it was much easier picking out the things I must not have in order to be happy first. Once you have created your list of must not haves, you can compare alternatives and start creating your list of must haves. Make sense?

Give it a try and see what you can come up with:

Must Haves:

Ex. Sense of humour ______________________

______________________ ______________________

______________________ ______________________

______________________ ______________________

Must Not Haves:

Ex. Smoker ______________________

______________________ ______________________

______________________ ______________________

______________________ ______________________

Many of us have never thought of what we truly need specifically in order to be happy, and how can we expect to find the perfect mate without a clear vision of who that may be? Completing this exercise above will help give you that clarity, and if you are not currently in a relationship, you can use this as a cheat sheet for upcoming dates. Staying focused on the details of what makes you happy is much easier when you have a list handy. Clarity is key!

If you are already in a relationship, this exercise will shed some light on which of your must haves are being met, and which of your must not haves are present. The more specific examples the better, because you'll be more prepared to have a constructive conversation with your partner about what is making you happy in your relationship and what needs work.

In this chapter we have discussed creating realistic visions of what a healthy relationship looks like, how communication within your relationships is not only important but absolutely vital for survival, and how none of the above matters if you don't have a loving, trusting, and fully accepting relationship with yourself first!

Any relationship can be salvaged, and this is including the most important relationship with yourself. Make the decision to make small changes, make little commitments such as to stop self-criticizing, and do your daily positive affirmations throughout the day. This little commitment will continue to grow, and you will find little improvements in your mood and life. That positive reinforcement will begin to create new commitments on top of the original two. Now you can add a few more self-improvement steps in your day. This growth and improvement will give you extra self-confidence, which will give you more motivation for self-improvement. This is a never ending merry-go-round of goodness! All it takes is one little step, and eventually the other foot will follow, and in time you will pick up momentum, which will continue on with you the rest of your life. Momentum only needs a little push to get started.

Consider this your push.

Conquering Fear

Fear makes people do crazy things, and it's one smart SOB too. It stealthily grows inside of us, and takes full control over everything that we do. It makes us destroy things we love, and somehow makes us sabotage ourselves in ways nothing else could. Fear makes alcohol look like a chump when it comes to making us act like a★★holes.

But how do we conquer it? Sometimes I wonder if it's even a real thing or if it's just a figment of our imagination that we create while we stew about things, like the boogie monster? If so, how in the hell do we conquer a make-believe boogie monster? Now I'm frightened.

When we discussed resentment we touched base on how fear is one of the main reasons we all settle in this life. The fear of losing what we have, losing who we love, and losing control over the situation are all very convincing reasons to avoid conflict and just leave things as-is, for fear the result might be worse than what we already have.

Everyone deals with self-talk throughout their day, and if you are anything like me, most of my inner chatter was fearful. There are constantly things in life that could go wrong, but I reached a point in my life where I wondered, "Does this worry actually accomplish anything, or make it less likely that things will go wrong?"

Once I clearly understood that my worry was the biggest waste of time imaginable, I was stumped on how to stop a habit that I have had literally for as long as I could remember. Remembering back to my childhood, I was never in a secure situation. I was always worried that my mom wouldn't have enough money to pay the bills, or that we would have to move again. These real-life stresses as a child were a legitimate reason to stress, even though the worries didn't help the situation. I believe my fear was simply a habit formed at a young age, and I internally established that it was a good method for survival. So I would continue this habit to ensure I continued to thrive. Even though it was rotting me from the inside out and I was a never-ending ball of stress regardless of how care-free my life was in reality.

I began doing research on cognitive therapy. As I explained earlier, cognitive therapy is a psychotherapy that states you can change the way you feel, by changing the way you think. Understanding the basics of brain function can be very helpful in changing the mental patterns that we all practise daily.

You cannot have any emotional reaction to an event until you have had a thought about it and given it meaning.

In many instances, it is not the event or thing that brings fear into our minds, but rather it is simply a meaning or thought that we have created about the event or thing. I read a story about an elderly gentlemen who drove his car onto train tracks and was hit by a train while countless cars watched helplessly. When the man was rescued from his car (thankfully uninjured) he was in great spirits and didn't seem bothered by the accident. He didn't know exactly what had happened, and when people explained that he was struck by a train, he was surprised, but still relaxed. Due to the fact that this man was senile and was not comprehending the severity of the situation, he had not given that accident any meaning. The meaning would have been the fuel for his anxiety and fear. Because he was unable to completely comprehend the severity of the situation, there was no fear or anxiety experienced.

In many cases our fear keeps us safe from such dangers as driving on train tracks, but how often does our fear hinder us when there are no true life-threatening dangers around? Think of your fear of tiny little spiders who are non-venomous. Why do we fear them? I'm scared to death of spiders, and I am completely aware that there is no real threat from them.

In theory, if we do not have that thought creating this non-life threatening danger, and do not give it meaning, we will not feel fear. Again, it sounds too simple to be possible, but that is the key. In most cases, the fears that we over-glorify throughout our days are almost never as bad as reality. I'll give you an example.

I lived a life of fear of years, and was partly a hypochondriac. If I had so much as a cough I'd look online and basically discover that I had some rare form of cancer. No matter what the symptom was, the self-diagnosis always ended up being cancer for some reason.

So the day comes that I contract a very rare infection in my breast implant (and this book finally gets juicy!) that had me down for the count for three weeks of excruciating pain, weakness, and mental fatigue. Then I have to be rushed down for emergency surgery. Then I'm walking around for two months with only one breast implant (1 A cup, 1 DD cup: *lovely*). Then I have to go back down for a second surgery. Then the recovery from that surgery. Did I mention this all occurred during the year of my wedding, and my last surgery occurred a week before my final wedding dress fitting? And I was two months into a strict fitness routine to lose weight for the wedding prior to this infection occurring.

Needless to say that was a legitimately stressful time, and a nightmare on Earth for most planet dwellers. But the thing was, it really wasn't that bad. Obviously it wasn't the most ideal situation, but when something serious happens with your health, or any other aspect of your life, you just get to work and do whatever needs to be done. But for the first two weeks of infection, I drove myself crazy with fear. I didn't know I would be having surgery, and I didn't even know the cause for my infection, and those unknowns became so incredibly scary and intimidating. The what-ifs were more than I could bear. I would spend hours looking online for possible outcomes, causes and worst case scenarios. Sure I may have a little something to worry about, but why feed your energy into that topic? Where focus goes, energy flows and so the more thought and meaning I put negatively into the situation, the more anxious and fearful I became.

By the third week of my infection I simply didn't have the physical energy to pour into this fearful cause, and with that I also realized that I was in control of how I was feeling. If I was feeling fearful it was because it was my *choice* to do so. And if I wanted to look through the situation from a more positive perception; then I could do that too. I put all my eggs in the bravery basket and began to move forward with a purpose. I would get through whatever in the hell was in my body and I would do it with a smile. It can always be worse, that much I promise you!

So I took control of what I could, let go of the things I couldn't, and marched on.

Every time I speak about this experience I start with, "It was the best thing that could have ever happened to me." When my friends and family pick their jaws up off the floor I explain: I lived a life ruled by fear, but when something truly threatening actually happened it wasn't as bad as I thought. It gave me confidence to see how well I handled myself, and it really brought out the best in my support system around me, making me feel extra loved and appreciative. And to this day I have let go of the fear of what is lurking around the corner in my life. I'm confident whatever it is, I am ready for it. I'm not going to waste my life worrying about what's to come, because then I miss out on what is important today. There is a whole lot of life to live, and you can only be one place at a time: in the past, the present, or the future. And I plan on seizing this moment, right now!

The Gist of It

Fear is only as strong as the energy that we focus on it. Fear requires significance to survive, and if we make the decision today to give up the daily trivial fears in our lives, we will be able to enjoy the simple pleasures that come to us. If we focus on all the things we fear, that is what will take over our lives. If we make the decision to be confident enough in ourselves to know that we can conquer whatever comes at us, we can begin to enjoy our lives without constantly looking over our shoulder at what could go wrong.

If sh★t happens, it happens. Deal with it. Don't waste your perfectly good life, wondering if something terrible might happen. Because what if it doesn't and you just wasted all your years thinking of the future? And so what if shit does hit the fan, what is so bad that you will never recover? Uncovering these fears is the first step in conquering them!

The Fix For It

I found that my fears were so convincing at times that I have a hard time shutting them up. So one day I grabbed a notepad and a pen and got creative. I wrote down some of my biggest fears in life, and when my list was complete I sat there and analyzed each one diligently.

Don't throw the book out the window — I can explain! It sounds counterproductive, but in most cases it's that fear of the unknown that is the biggest fear of them all. So if we write down the worst possible scenarios in our mind, and then try to break them down one-by-one, it proves that most of these fears are things that we are creating, and they aren't really worth your time entertaining them.

So I began to dig deeper and deeper into my fears and was able to laugh at the majority of them, once I had gotten to the bottom of them. Let's see an example.

Let's say my fear is this book flopping miserably. Pretend I don't even sell a single copy outside of my immediate family. Let's allow that fear to be tested below:

What's your fear?

> My book failing miserably

Then what would happen?

> Well, I would have wasted my time, and everyone would think I'm a failure.

Then what would happen?

Well, people could talk about me behind my back and not want to be my friend anymore.

Then what would happen?

Well they kind of sound like terrible friends if they are doing that anyway.

So I guess I'd find new friends? I'd still be proud that I at least tried to follow my dreams — regardless of the outcome!

So that one only took me three progressions to see that my fear of this book failing isn't really worth a damn thing. But how many people do you know give up on dreams for fear of failing in it?

I still battle a fear of heights, but in the past few months I have gone rappelling 30 feet down a building and volunteered to go into a fire truck bucket which took me up 135ft in the air. Crazy right? To most I may sound like a sucker for punishment, but I am finding the more I push my limits, the less affected I am by my fears. Plus I build confidence with each act of bravery I display, which is a bonus!

I want to physically show myself that fear will not get the best of me. That can go for anything, even spiders (yuck!). Just write down a few fears, critique them logically, and maybe come up with a few little challenges that you can do to push the limits of your fear. You don't have to go 135ft in the air, but you could go into a pet store and look at a giant pet spider for a few minutes and try to find something not horrifying about it? Baby steps!

On a blank piece of paper write down the following questions:

1. What is your fear?

2. What would happen if this fear came true? (Ask as many times as it takes until you've found peace with it)

3. What could you do to limit this fear's control over you? (E.g. Hold a snake, go zip lining, find a way to push your limit!)

Fear cannot control you, only YOU can control you.

If there is something in your life you're sick of being afraid of, challenge it! Desensitize yourself to things that you have negative associations with. Fear is a negative feeling that we can control, so why would we opt to keep it in our lives? Take the first step, no matter how small it may be, and take one of those fears off of your list. Life is waiting!

Another way to take the sting out of fears is preparing for them. Now I'm not suggesting you go out and build a bomb shelter because you've gone cray-cray and are fearful of an alien takeover. But what I'm saying is, there are some fears in your life that have validity, or are a reasonable cause for some anxiety, and can be prepared for in advance to lessen the damage of the fear.

Perfect example: public speaking.

There are people that actually list the fear of public speaking above death. Which technically means they would choose *death* over public speaking. WTF? I have friends who have dreaded their best friend's wedding simply due to the fact they knew being Maid of Honour required a speech!

So when we recognize a fear like this, we have a choice: we can feed into this fear and essentially let it run our experience, or we can use it as fuel. Taking a negative and turning it into a positive. How do we do it? We *prepare.* We can take the time we have, and prepare the greatest speech known to man, and practise the hell out of it. And rehearse it in front of a few close friends (desensitize) and repeat it enough so that you could practically do it in your sleep. Would that not take some of the fear out of the equation? Sure you still have to speak in front of people, but preparing for something mentally assures us, and makes things more manageable.

Am I suggesting that preparing is going to make this daunting task a joy for you? No, it's probably still going to suck because you hate public speaking. If you can build the confidence in yourself and your speech and at least know it's going to be stellar, however, that is how you take fear and make it work for you. The fear is still there, but it is going to fuel you to do a much better job. Rather than overwhelming you and causing you to be an anxious, sweaty mess — when you *should* be dealing with your anxious, sweaty bride-to-be!

So three steps to free yourself of fears (or at least simmer them down!):

1. Recognize whether the fear is real, or just something you're creating or blowing out of proportion.

2. Desensitize yourself of it by questioning it, and putting yourself in uncomfortable situations with it.

3. Prepare for it. Use your fear as fuel and strengthen yourself and your surroundings so you aren't victim to the fear. Keep a secret stash of cash under your mattress, practice cooking the meal before inviting Mr. Wonderful over, and prepare that fabulous speech already! When you're already prepared for a worst case scenario, what is there left to fear?

We've all heard the saying "There is nothing to fear but fear itself" but why don't we apply that into our daily lives?

Life is meant to be lived, not feared. Whatever the case may be, have the confidence in yourself, your life, and the people you've picked to share your life with you; to know that everything will be alright. Show fear who's boss, and it'll be running out the front door with its tail tucked between its legs in no time!

No fear.

Finding Faith

Now let me begin with saying, I'm the last person on Earth that is going to write a chapter about God, how he's real, and how you're all burning in hell if you don't agree with me. Nope, that's not me. I've had a long and interesting relationship with religion, and I've butted heads on occasion with my mother when my plans didn't exactly line up with (her) "Big Man Upstairs'."

I recall reaching the religion chapter in a self-help book I was reading and thought about skipping over it. I was actually a little annoyed it was even included, because I subconsciously held resentments against all organized religions. But a day came when I realized spiritual well-being is just as important as physical or mental well-being. Without it you are lost in this world.

I am not saying religion is necessary, I'm saying *faith* is necessary. Without faith, you couldn't leave your bed. Think about it: without certainty and faith, how could you be sure a car wasn't going to cross the centre line of the road and hit you? Or how could you be sure that the roof of your office won't come crashing down on you? What about being struck by lightning? How can you be sure that won't happen? If we didn't have faith that these things weren't going to happen, how would we ever live our lives? We'd be consumed with fear and we would live our lives hiding under our bed. Pending that didn't crash down on us too?

These are basic examples of things we have faith in, so we do not fear the outcomes or overanalyze them. If we can broaden our horizons to bigger and more specific things in our day, and apply faith, we will find an entirely different world around us.

I personally feel every individual has their own right to believe whatever they want, and as passionately as they wish. If you want to worship Starbucks, I am not one to judge. Just as long as you aren't judging others, or hurting anyone in the process!

There was a long period of time where I went out of my way to be an Atheist and not believe in anything at all. Religion was too structured and demanding, and my values didn't jive with the lessons I was being preached. I figured I would just do my own thing, be a good person, and spread love and joy. It sounded good enough to me.

But while I was practicing this, something didn't feel quite right, and I felt incomplete in a sense. I knew I didn't need to believe in God because I was afraid of dying, and needed a safe place to go when I was all done here on Earth, but I did realize something significant: I needed to believe in *something* to feel good in my life. I needed to know with certainty that my life had purpose, and I had some form of destiny to accomplish. Faith gives each person a higher calling, and that sense of belonging to a cause is impossible to describe.

Now in hindsight I understand why that is, and I will get to it soon, but in that moment I was quite puzzled at this yearning for faith. I truly felt I needed faith in *something* to ease my troubled mind. There are things that happen in this lifetime that we simply cannot fathom as mere mortals, and we need to have faith that things happen for a reason, and that everything will be OK in time. That is where this faith, or trust, comes in to save the day.

Life would be pretty disappointing if we truly believed that our purpose in life was to simply roam around for about 60-100 years, and then die. I'd probably just give up right now if that were true! And especially in those low times in our life, when we are down and out and feel that we have no one to turn to — that is where this faith is needed above all else. Like a parachute, we all need to have that back up chute 'in case of emergency' in life. That simple knowing that there is something bigger than yourself at play, is often enough to pick up the pieces and move on. Without it you would have nothing and would feel terribly alone.

Knowing that your life is guided by something bigger than you makes it possible to see things for what they are, and gives you meaning to your life. If you saw every negative event as a test rather than just a horrible day, would you react differently? It would certainly give you extra fuel not to give up. When I began living with my higher calling in mind, my world shifted completely. I analyze what things mean now rather than fly off of emotion, and I can find meaning in any situation, good or bad. If some unplanned mishap occurs, rather than feeling frustrated, I feel determined to crush this obstacle immediately. And when I do, I chuckle to myself thinking "Nice one, universe. You're always keeping me on my toes!" and move on to the next moment. I know everything that happens is happening for a reason, and my role in that situation is to deal with it to the best of my ability. Not sit on the floor and cry about how hard and unfair life is. There is always a lesson to be learned. And if the same lesson keeps repeating again and again in your life, then clearly you're not getting that message, and the universe will continue to put it in your lap until you change your ways, which will change this pattern.

Just like the balance of Yin and Yang, faith is the light to fear's darkness.

Faith is the absence of fear, and without faith, fear is inevitable. So it comes to no shock to me that the more faith I apply in my life, the less fear I experience. Fear always involves worry, and worrying is like praying for something bad to happen. Having faith and giving thanks to the universe, or whichever God you believe in, is how you pray for good things to happen! It's that simple. Have faith and watch your life transform.

Faith and fear are both figments of our imagination. **Fear is the image of how terrible things could be, and faith is the image of how wonderful it could be**. You have the choice to see through either perspectives, so why wouldn't you choose to live an enchanted life full of faith? Plus, everything you think is put out into the universe and, according to the law of attraction, if you are thinking negative thoughts, negative things will be attracted back to you. If you choose to think positive thoughts full of faith then positive and wonderful things will be attracted to you and your life.

Being grateful for every little thing is a great way to start building your faith. Stop seeing things as good luck, and start seeing them as gifts in your life from the universe (or God). I do not believe in coincidence, I feel that every little thing that happens to you happened for a reason. If your car breaks down, there is a reason you weren't supposed to be at work on time. If a boyfriend breaks your heart, there is someone else much better suited to you waiting for you in this life. Every little thing, down to spilling coffee on your shirt, happens with intention, and your reactions to these adversities can clearly change the outcome of these intentions.

Some days you feel like nothing can go right, and you've got to learn to ask yourself, "What am I supposed to be learning from this day?" If you can look at things less emotionally, and more analytically, you may find lessons that you have been missing your entire life. Possibly the lesson is to just learn to breathe and be appreciative for the things going great in your life, even when a lot of things seem to be going not-so-great! Even that statement alone needs analyzing: why do you perceive things as going not-so-great? Because they weren't what you expected?

What screws us up most in life is the picture in our head of how it is supposed to be.

If you can put your expectations aside, and simply view your life for what it is in this moment, we've all got it pretty great! Focusing on the silver lining is an acquired skill that we all need to sharpen. With unlimited optimism, nothing can ever get you down. Put your focus on the good, and work hard to improve the areas in your life that are lacking. It never has to be more complicated than that.

I am a huge supporter of meditation, which I believe to be a critical tool in building your relationship not only with yourself, but to the universe and spiritual realm of this world. Prior to meditation I relied on medication for ADHD and depression. I tried to get off the medications, but I would be a mess with scattered thoughts and my anxiety and stress would return almost immediately. I was fed up with the side effects, and I wanted to find balance more naturally. I had been taking these medications for over two years, and I didn't know if it was possible to ever get completely off of them.

After reading and researching, I decided that I needed to start meditating regularly, so I began meditating once or twice a day, and really put the effort in to get in touch with my mind and body and find some balance. Within three weeks I was off both my medications, and haven't taken them since. I'm not saying that medication is the enemy here, but what if we could find peace from within and heal our own minds? What if we could be relying on meditation rather than medication to release us from the grips of depression, anxiety and attention deficit disorders? Wouldn't it be worth a try? I thought so, and I'm so glad I did!

I will explain more about my introduction to meditation in the next chapter, 'Perceptions,' as I had an interesting journey, thinking it had to be a certain way; in reality you can meditate in whatever way works for you. Maybe that's listening to some guided meditation, or lying on a beach and listening to the waves crash. Perhaps it's sitting in complete silence and listening to your breathing. Maybe you're not listening to anything and simply looking deep within for something. The result is what is important and the result is relaxing your mind and retreating to a higher place within yourself to connect and be. It's that simple. When you feel this connection for the first time it is incredible. And it's something you can always rely on. Feeling overwhelmed or stressed about something? Meditate. Need answers for a problem and you consciously can't figure it out? Meditate. Need a perfect way to start your day with clarity and purpose? Meditate! You seeing a pattern here? Meditation is the fix for almost all of life's problems. I realize that's quite a statement, but I also believe it's true.

You can't think clearly when you are not spiritually grounded, so by meditating you can calm your mind and ease your nerves, and when you are done with your meditation, if you haven't come to a conclusion throughout the process, then you will at least have the clearest mind possible to revisit the issue with new eyes, and hopefully new solutions. When you have found an unlimited source of peace from within, you can conquer any obstacle that appears before you.

Some find this peace at church, surrounded by like-minded people, and they find that peace they are seeking, and while they pray they can connect with themselves and with their higher power. Other people prefer going to yoga, and they crave that relaxed feeling they experience afterwards. It doesn't matter what your outlet is, just so long as you are connecting on a spiritual level to something or someone, especially yourself.

Maybe you're like me who didn't really fit into any particular religion and just want to believe that there is *something* out there, and that there are energies out in the world that you feel, but can't necessarily explain. There is nothing wrong with that either, as we all must dig deep and find that faith, because without it we will be filled with fear instead.

I resisted religion and spiritual connection for years, because of negative experiences growing up within a church. Unfortunately my resistance kept me from any form of inner balance, and during hard times when I really could have used it. I'm not sure there is ever a time when you couldn't use more inner peace, but I just know I was quite a mess back then. Once I realized that I required spiritual connection, I began searching for a title or fixed religion that I could belong to. I read books on Buddhists and loved everything they were saying. And while I feel I relate to their beliefs the best, I still like to consider myself my own being with my own spiritual connection to the universe. I personally saw a hindrance of inner peace with the labelling and rules of different religions, so I am currently simply a student of the universe. I meditate, practice affirmations and gratitude, and simply focus on the lessons that the universe puts in my path daily.

Rather than living my life as a human being having a spiritual experience, I like to imagine I'm a spiritual being having a human experience!

There might still be some old versions of me out there, thinking this is total bologna, but I assure you that without my spiritual awakening and daily strengthening, there would be no transformation within myself and my life. That is an absolute fact for me. Gratitude is one of the strongest catalysts for change in your life, because when you truly become grateful for every little thing that is going well in your life, it becomes so much easier to deal with the few things that are complicating your journey. I used to spend almost all of my time focusing on the things that weren't going right and would ignore all of the good in my life. It was the only way I knew how to process life's events. But I quickly learned through practise in positive affirmations and gratitude, that your focus on the good or bad is a choice only you can make for yourself. No matter how many unplanned issues arise, you can always choose to be grateful for what is good. You can choose to only think and speak in ways that are empowering to you and to everyone around you. It's all a choice. Do you want to empower or disempower yourself and the ones around you?

I heard a wonderful analogy regarding this choice of ours we make daily. When it comes to our thoughts and outlooks on life, we have something similar to a large buffet of options. So imagine you're standing in line for your buffet breakfast. But rather than food on the platters, they are thoughts and perceptions of how your day is going to go and what you will think. There are options in front of you that will nourish you and make you feel good, and then there are options that will make you feel uneasy, sick, and unhappy. You've got an empty plate in your hands, and it is entirely your choice on which options you want to take throughout the day! Will you willingly choose options that will harm you? Or will you make the choice to make excellent choices for the day, and enjoy the abundance of goodness that you will carry around with you the entire day? Maybe you even just start with replacing a few bad options with better ones, and feel that little difference in the day. And with that positive influence, you may want even more the next day. The point is, no one else is serving these options to you, you've got to go for what you want out of the day and grasp it!

Just as we can control what we choose to feel in this life, we have full control over what we believe in as well. There are two types of people in this world: people who don't believe anything is a miracle, and people who think everything is a miracle. We can decide to be jaded, not believe in anything, and simply believe that crazy things happen in this life out of mere coincidence. Or we can decide to believe in whatever we are feeling. The best advice I ever heard about developing your belief system is to always remain a skeptic. What this means is, don't jump into a religion or belief because your family or friends recommend it, and then stick with it because you made your choice and now you must live with it. Shop around and follow your heart. Some beliefs may not make sense to you, and others may make complete sense to you. Don't go with what everyone else is doing to avoid discomfort or seclusion, make your own path and follow your heart. The path to spiritual enlightenment is not the path most travelled, and is often a different path for different people, and there is nothing wrong with that. Maybe what works for me and makes me content, doesn't work for you. And vice versa. The important thing about faith is that it is all yours. Be a skeptic and decide for yourself what makes you feel good. Don't believe what anyone else tells you about your spiritual journey, believe what your heart tells you! It will never lead you astray.

Your faith can be whatever you need it to be to feel balance from within. I'm sure many people could read this chapter and think, "She's not talking to the universe, she's talking to God," and for them maybe that's exactly what I'm doing. But in my case, that label doesn't do me any justice. I know what I feel, and I love what I feel, and that is how I make my decisions in this life. If I am doing something unethical, I feel that weight in my subconscious because I am betraying my own beliefs and morals. I live a healthy, rich life full of love and compassion for others, and inspiring others to live a healthy and inspired life is my life's purpose. I feel it's my destiny, and one that the universe has put at my feet. I have faith in what I feel, because what I feel is real to me. And what you feel is real to you too. It's just about recognizing what you feel, and what you require for fulfillment and a balanced life.

When you put spirituality at the top of your priorities, you find an inner calm that is nothing short of a miracle in this life. That peace is what makes you extra capable to tackle some of life's most difficult tests. When your daily routine neglects grounding your body and mind, you are left floating above the ground completely consumed by life's demands. When you have faith in your life and know with certainty that every missed opportunity happens for a reason, you spend less time mourning the unexpected turn of events, and more time celebrating what you currently have and plotting out how to make the next goal come true.

Any strong tree has a broad base and deep roots, right? Those roots go deep into the soil, and make it so that nothing above the ground could ever knock it over, because it is too steady. Meditation, affirmations and gratitude are ways that we can strengthen and deepen our roots within our lives. These practises make us stronger spiritually and mentally. How strong would a big, thick tree be with no roots? It could be knocked over with a feather. I don't know about you, but I've certainly felt that frail in the past, just hoping nothing would go wrong because I just couldn't possibly handle another disappointment at that time. Had I known then what I know now, I would have begun meditating and connecting spiritually with myself at the first sign of distress, and then I'd be ready for battle regardless of what comes in my path.

The body-mind-spirit connection is no myth, there is a real connection between these elements of our being. So much so that while I was training for my first-ever fitness competition, I was instructed by my personal trainer to make the next week's focus solely on my mental and spiritual strength. I had to do this because without the mental and spiritual strength and conditioning, I could never stick to the physical regime, and definitely could not handle the extremes within this sport. I wouldn't have the mental endurance to deal with the criticism of my body, the demanding hours, and the dedication required to push through the tough days of my contest preparation. I could build my physical strength all I wanted, but like a tree, I needed something to keep me resilient and grounded. So I dug my roots deep into the ground below me, and now the sacrifices required to succeed in this sport all make sense, and I maintain a grounded mind and spirit daily to make sure I can handle the stress of competition. This is not something you can skip for a day, it must be consistent and never ending, like your own self-improvement.

We need physical, emotional, *and* spiritual balance to achieve true happiness. If one section is lacking, they will all suffer. It's like only being as strong as your weakest link, you need to ensure you have built strength in all three areas before you can ever truly feel fulfilled in life. Faith is something you acquire when you practise this body-mind-spirit connection daily. It begins as something foreign that you are trying out, and it feels forced, but in time it becomes so natural, and eventually you wonder how you ever lived without it. And the more faith you have in your life, the less room for fear!

The less fear in your life; the more positive your thoughts will be, which will inevitably bring more prosperity into your life. The law of attraction is the idea that like attracts like, and if you think positive thoughts you will receive positivity in your life. But if your thoughts are clouded with negativity and fear, that is what you will attract instead.

What you think, you become
-Buddha

When I spent my life in fear and worry, I continually ran into more situations that increased my fear and worry. When I decided to make this change, I gave up that fear and worry, and replaced it with faith and positivity, and my life has never been the same since.

Does this mean bad things will stop happening to you? No, that is definitely not what it means. Life will still occur, pain will be felt, but with a positive outlook you can see beyond the pain, and see the lessons within the pain. You take something from every situation, and so you are not suffering in vain, like you are now. Currently if you feel pain, it is simply a byproduct of something that has occurred in your life, or something that hasn't met your expectation. And we live in this pain until we have distracted ourselves with food, TV, Facebook, or friends. Distracting yourself from pain will not take it away, and it certainly will not prevent it in the future. Having faith gives you the ability to see the purpose behind each struggle, and know that it is happening for a reason. Once you have identified the purpose of the adversity, you can figure out how it will serve in making you a stronger, more enlightened individual. And who doesn't want that?

The idea of something "bad" happening is simply a state of mind too. If life was perfect we would all be incredibly bored all the time. Feeling pain and facing adversity is a sign that we are alive; the only people on this planet who do not face daily adversity are buried deep beneath the soil. The universe will continue to test you until the day you die, and it is up to you on whether or not you want to continue on the path you are currently on, and repeat your old patterns or whether you want to finally learn the lessons you are being provided. Growing is a part of life, and an important key in you reaching your destiny.

Have faith that all is well in your world, and show appreciation daily for all the things in your life that you love. And then spend time loving the things in your life that bring you grief. Each and every thing in our life is there for a reason, and you must show gratitude for them all. Be thankful that you have a mortgage payment, because it means that you own a home. Be thankful to that person who has cut you off in traffic, because they are teaching you to be a more patient person. Be thankful to the rain, because without it nothing could ever grow, and we would live in a barren desert.

Just be grateful. Just be loving. Just be kind.

And the universe will be grateful, loving, and kind to you.

The Gist of It

Having faith does not necessarily involve an organized religion or any guidelines at all, but rather a trust in the universe that you live in, and the life that you are living. Learn to trust this life, and know with certainty that anything that happens or doesn't happen, occurs for a reason or for a greater good, even if we can't quite figure it out in the moment. This trust brings a flow into our lives, and attracts love and prosperity to us. We must surrender to this life and have faith in our life's outcomes.

Faith is the opposite of fear, and there is only so much room in your life to accommodate both. If your life is filled with faith, it leaves no room for fear. Both faith and fear are figments of our imagination: one is the image of how terrible our lives could become, and the other is the image of how wonderful our lives could become. Make the choice to imagine the wonders of this world, and they will come to you. You will attract positivity and light into your life by thinking positive thoughts. Remember: what you think, you become.

Having faith does not make you immune to the pains and woes of life, but it gives you a deeper understanding of the "big picture." You have the choice to see your reality in any way you choose, because your reality is simply what you focus on. If you only focus on the hardships, life will seem cold and unfair, but if you focus on all of the wonderful blessings in your life, you will feel fulfilled and blessed. It is only natural that we must learn and experience the things that we love, and the things that we do not love in this life, or how else would we know what we prefer? Adversity brings adventure into our lives, and it is all about how we perceive our struggles. If we can make the choice to see each obstacle in our lives as a test, rather than bad luck, we can strive for great performances and celebrate our victories. But if we do not see the purpose in our pain, then we are suffering in vain and nothing can ever be gained from that experience. Perception is everything. This includes faith.

The good news is: you already have a varying degree of faith, or you would not feel comfortable getting out of bed. You could spend all day worried about the roof caving in above you, being struck by lightning, or a car crossing the middle line on the road you are driving on, but you don't because you have enough faith to get you through those potentials.

Identifying that we do currently have faith is a beautiful tool in strengthening this trust within ourselves and the universe. Because once you have something, it is simply a matter of nurturing it and watching it grow stronger and stronger each day. We all have faith within us, it is simply putting the time and effort into nurturing this life-altering change in perception, and practising it every day until it becomes second nature.

We nurture our faith by practising daily meditation, gratitude, and affirmations. Every single day for the rest of our lives.

Faith is just like a muscle: you wouldn't go to the gym, build glorious muscles, and then quit as soon as you've built the body you're looking for right? Because what would happen next? Your hard-earned muscles would eventually fade. It is something that must be worked on daily if you want to maintain muscles, or faith, or pretty much anything worth having in this life.

Faith is something you can choose to have this very moment, while you are sitting there holding this book. Talk about fate: you picked out this book yourself, and now you are reading these pages and you're feeling this connection. This connection is you connecting with the universe, and accepting that coincidences do not exist, and that everything on this Earth happens for a reason. There is a purpose behind every single thing that happens in your day, and when you begin to tune into these tiny miracles, you'll be amazed at the wonder of it all.

The simplest example just happened yesterday to me. I was wondering about my car loan, and how much I had owing on it. Not a sound was even made out loud, but I wondered how to find this information, I wasn't even sure how to contact the provider for my loan, because it had just recently changed a few months back due to a business acquisition. I quickly forgot about it and got back to work. I come home that day from work to find an envelope with my name on it, from the lenders of my loan. They had sent me a quarterly statement of how much I had contributed and how much I still owed on my loan. Just as easy as that. This was the first time I had ever been sent a statement in the almost three years I owned my car. And just like that, the universe delivered it to me. I sincerely thanked the universe for sharing this information with me, and continued on with my perfect day.

Some people could roll their eyes and think, "That was just a coincidence" but what makes them right? Why are they so sure that this is not the universe giving me what I asked for? This is the beauty of this life we live: we have options. We can decide to perceive things in any way we choose, and one event can mean many different things to many different people. It's a wonderful thing, really.

So why not make the decision today, in this moment, that you will see the wonders of the world from this point on? You can choose to believe that our lives are guided by something greater than us. So take some of that pressure off of your own shoulders and know that you are destined to be what you become. Work with faith: meaning envision what you truly desire, know with faith that this dream will come true, and work your butt off to achieve it. Don't spend too much time being concerned with *how* it will be achieved, because the universe will figure that out for you. The important thing is feeling with all certainty that it will happen, and then follow through with some serious action.

Let's get to our faith-filled game plan!

The Fix For It

The most important thing to realize when it comes to living with faith, is recognizing that you already have it within you. When we were small children we saw the world through eyes with absolutely no filters. There was no influence yet in our minds, and we were free to dream big, without any cares in the world. We didn't fear criticism from our peers if we wanted to be a unicorn when we grew up, we simply knew that this was our destiny. But over time we became so influenced by social standards, and became educated on what was acceptable, and then vowed to never leave those boundaries again for fear of seclusion from society.

I am suggesting we tear those walls down, and begin to live our lives with passion and the belief that anything is possible. We must have trust in our lives to accept the hardships as simply challenges set out for our own self-improvement. Everything happens for a reason, and there is always a lesson to be learned, so we must begin to see life through those vulnerable, believing eyes again.

Acceptance of life, with all of its quirks and surprises, will be your essential first step to living a life driven with faith and passion.

When you begin to accept this life for what it is, you can begin to build your faith. Establishing what you currently own in the faith department will be a healthy second step. Identify what you believe, and where you are finding difficulty. We are creatures of habit, so when changes begin to occur it is only natural that our minds will begin to resist. Our minds will resist new beliefs because it is uncharted territory for us, and it is our conscious duty to analyze why we are feeling this way. Question yourself and analyze the answers you have.

Recently while looking through real estate with my husband I began to insist we look for less expensive homes, and made a comment along the lines of, "I would never approve of us buying a home that grand." We were looking at extravagant real estate as a way to manifest prosperity into our lives, so for me to make that comment was very counterproductive. My husband asked me why not, and I caught myself resisting the process. I had a road block mentally, but wasn't sure why. In reality, if we had millions of dollars, why wouldn't I want a grand, beautiful home? There was absolutely no reason, except for my fears that we couldn't achieve this dream. My fear made me second-guess our abilities to achieve our goals, and a by-product of that belief was to lower my standards to make them more achievable. If I had continued to believe in that, I would ultimately limit our potential by telling the universe we couldn't have the grander home. With change, often comes resistance. But it is up to each and every one of us to fight this resistance, and to assure ourselves that "Yes I do deserve this. Thank you universe for putting this into my life".

When we have begun to conquer some of our own doubts, we can begin embracing the idea of manifesting and attracting prosperity with our own positivity. Much of this attraction occurs when you begin to develop a relationship with whatever is your source of faith. For some, this may be God, and for others it may be something different. I prefer to speak to the divine powers within the universe, whatever they may be. So pick what you believe in, and then work hard to establish a relationship built on trust and love. Just like human relationships, these spiritual relationships will involve work and communication. We must connect to the spiritual realm so that we are comfortable asking for things that we desire in life. You will never receive items you never ask for.

Thank the universe daily for all of the goodness it has placed into your life, and thank the Universe for putting the hardships into your life too. Without those struggles you wouldn't be nearly as strong and resilient as you are today. Good is not appreciated without the bad, because you will never have anything to compare it to, to know how good it really is. Start to see the good in every person, place and event that occurs in your life, because if you look hard enough, it is always there. There is always something you can take from a situation, a lesson you can learn, or a message to share. The challenge is getting efficient at recognizing the silver linings, and seeing life with a more unbiased, analytical observation. When you know that something has happened for a reason, you begin searching for these reasons. When you find the reasons, you can learn from them. When you learn from your past, you can begin to change your patterns to avoid more pain in the future. This is where change begins!

In order to keep track of changes and progress, begin journaling every single day. Write down how you felt throughout the day, journal any ideas that pop up throughout the day, and write down your affirmations. This is more important than you think, because it is this daily accountability of journaling that will keep you on track. Just like anything else, if you don't use it, you lose it. If you aren't working every single day on your spiritual well-being, then it will taper off slowly, and you will eventually become unbalanced again. My personal journal includes all areas of my life and well-being, but if you'd prefer to keep separate ones for physical, mental, and spiritual, then that is your choice to make. You know what will work best for you.

At the beginning for me, this felt like a chore and I didn't want to begin. I felt it was silly and a waste of time. But when I finally did give it a chance, I realized it was nothing like doing a chore. The more I wrote in my journal, the more satisfaction and pride I found in my efforts. I felt so proud the first day I had recorded all of my meals, workouts, and research I had completed. I wrote down all of the things I researched that day for my mental growth, all the meditations, affirmations and gratitude I exercised for my spiritual growth, and I tracked my food, workouts and sleep for my physical growth. This way, if I am ever looking for explanations for my mood or performance, I can go back and look. Many times I'll realize I didn't meditate that day, or I will look at my food journal for inconsistencies. By having all of my work summarized for me at my fingertips, I can begin analyzing my efforts when I am not seeing a desired result. It is quite the resource when you have invested a solid amount of time into building a daily journal.

It also makes you accountable for your actions. If you haven't meditated in three days, that's all in your journal. If you want to eat something that you know is not on your diet plan, you've got to write it down and make it real. Make it permanent in your records. You can't deny it any longer, you will become accountable for how much work you are putting into your day and it'll all be there for you to read any time you want. This is a great place to track your spiritual work such as gratitude and affirmations too.

Let's dive into the world of affirmations while we are here, shall we? As we discussed previously, for an affirmation to be effective, it needs to be present tense, positive, personal and specific. Affirmations can be anything from "My income is constantly increasing," to "I live in my dream house, which I can easily afford," to "I am married to the man/woman of my dreams," to "I am always succeeding," to "I cherish this day, this moment, right now." It can literally be anything that you wish it to be, and make many of them. These little statements will send a frequency out into the universe to let the universe know this is what you want.

Affirmations must be in the present tense because if we keep them in the future, the universe will take that information and will give you exactly what you're asking for: for the goal or dream to always be in your future. If you say your affirmations in present tense, the Universe understands that you are ready for the goods right now. The trick is to act as though you already have what it is that you dream of having, and live with that fulfillment and excitement for all the good in your life. Be thankful for that big promotion you've been waiting for, as though you already have it. If you want to be a movie star, sign some portraits of yourself and keep them in your pocket, as if people are already asking for your autograph.

Technically every thought you have throughout a day is an affirmation, and that is why every thought we have must be positive. If you are focusing on all the negatives in your life and everything you're lacking, that is all that will continue to be attracted to your life. If you create a few affirmations and repeat them a handful of times throughout the day, but every other thought throughout your day is negative, the results are not going to be as dramatic. At first this is going to be very difficult, you'll probably be shocked with how many negative thoughts come up in a day, but when they come up simply dismiss them and replace them with a positive thought. Learn to love your enemy and appreciate your struggles, and life will begin to bring you more of what you desire.

It is important to also understand that affirmations will feel funny at first to say, and will seem so unrealistic at times. And that is because they are in a sense: if affirmations weren't made up then we wouldn't need to say them now would we? They would be facts about what we already have. But if you can embrace this process and really go for it, you'll be amazed at the results. Hard work will always be involved in accomplishing your goals and dreams, but having the universe there as your ally will always help expedite the process. Have faith that you are putting it out there, and then bust your ass to achieve it, and in time you will see the results. Just remember to give yourself the time, and be patient. Nothing worth having ever comes too easy, and you'll have to accept the process as is, and have faith it will all work out, regardless of speed bumps. Look for the lessons when you face adversity in your journey, and love and appreciate them. Then just dust yourself off, and get back to work.

I have read multiple stories of famous actors and athletes who have been known to walk around like they were famous and successful long before they ever made a career of their passions. It was that confidence and knowing that their dreams would realize that brought them the amazing levels of success that they share today. Confidence triggers the law of attraction to deliver our dreams to us, and it brings out the best in us because the dreams feel so real that we are willing to sacrifice anything and everything to make our dreams a reality. You can dream all you want, but the end result will require work with faith. Have faith that your dreams will come true (with all certainty) and then work as hard as you possibly can to make it so. While you are working to achieve your goals, try not to focus on the process too much. Do the work, but do not become consumed with exactly how your dream must come to fruition. Remind yourself that the universe will have a better plan for you than you do, always!

Another method of this visualization is creating an 'inspiration board.' This is simply a collage of all of the things you dream for in life. They can be as crazy as you would like. There are no rules or limits; it is simply a board that visually displays what you would like to have, regardless of price tag, reality, or greed. Go through magazines, the Internet, and real estate listings and get those images printed out and pasted to a poster board. Having a visual cue for your mind will not only motivate you beyond your wildest dreams, but it will also subliminally send messages to yourself about what you want. It will also put something concrete out into the universe so that it knows what you would love in your life. Be sure to hang it somewhere you frequently visit so that you see it often. When you look at it, feel as though you already have all of the things on the board. Let it excite and inspire you, then watch them appear in your life. (Just make sure you're putting in the hard work required to earn them.)

Trying these methods involve applying your faith into your practise. Without faith, you won't give these a chance, and if you're struggling with these concepts, ask yourself: what do you have to lose? You must be open and willing to receive the abundance of goodness in this world, and you must believe that the universe will deliver it to you. You can't expect it overnight, so please don't quit too soon. It happens all too often that people give up just before they have broken through the surface of their dreams. Results will come when they are earned, and not a moment sooner. If you're feeling uneasy because you don't feel you have a close enough relationship with the universe, you'll need to develop a relationship with it.

As I mentioned earlier in this chapter, the most effective ways I have found to build my faith and relationship with the universe is through meditation and showing gratitude. These processes can be done separately or together. Meditation is any time that you are focusing solely on your body-mind-spirit connection, so there is no reason you can't give thanks to the universe while doing this. I like to show gratitude for the littlest things, because the more splendour you can find in your life, the better. Like how about the fact that we all need oxygen to survive, and there is an abundance on Earth, and it's free. Have you ever considered how incredibly lucky we are for this? We take a breath, and we know that there will be another oxygen filled breath waiting for us after we exhale. How wonderful that we do not have to worry about such things. Be thankful for your health. Be thankful for every little thing that is going right in your life. Be thankful for the things *not* going right in your life, because they are teaching you to be a stronger, patient, and more resilient survivor.

List a few things below that you are thankful for:

____

____

____

____

____

____

____

____

____

Every day try to write down five things that you are grateful for, and make sure every day you're writing down different things. You might think this sounds impossible, but think of all the millions of things that are good in our lives. You might have to get creative, but that's the whole point. You must train your mind to recognize the things that you are grateful for every day. The more naturally flowing your gratitude can be, the happier you will feel every single day. You'll be one step closer to enlightenment!

Meditate as often as you can, because nothing will make you feel better. I love meditating when I first wake up, before I go to sleep, and any time I am feeling anxious or tense. Mediation is something you can do anywhere, at any time, and it will always benefit you. The important thing is not *how* you meditate; it is simply that you make the time for it. If you're not sure where to start, search online for some guided meditations, and they will walk you through a meditation. There are guided meditations for relaxation, prosperity, growth, inner child healing, gratitude: pretty much anything you can think of. So identify something you'd like to focus on, and give it a try. You won't regret it!

We all have faith within us, and it is simply a matter of identifying what we currently have, applying it out into our daily behaviour, and building a stronger relationship with your spiritual self, and whatever divine energy you believe in. Affirmations, gratitude and meditation are your building blocks for getting yourself as grounded as possible, and with your roots deeply nestled in the soil below you, you will be stronger than ever. There will be no need for fear, and with that freedom there are absolutely no limits to what you can achieve in this life.

Have faith in yourself, your life, and your destiny — and watch the miracles appear one by one.

Shifting Perception

Perception has been mentioned between the lines of this entire book, and why do you think this is? I believe that perception is the most important thing in our lives. No, that was not a typo. I truly believe it is!

Health, money, friends: with or without these various wants and needs, we can still maintain happiness. It all comes down to our perception of life. Every emotion that we feel has little to nothing to do with the experiences that we face, but rather the association we have made and the meaning that we perceive in these experiences.

The classic glass half full or half empty comes to mind. The concept is so simple, and so accurate. Which outlook would make you feel happier and more fulfilled? Probably thinking that the glass was half full correct? So why is it that we can't look at life this way? Even if your life is in ruins and literally half of your life is a disaster in the current moment, remember to be honest with yourself and don't forget the things going right. Health, home, food, friends: why can't we look at that as "Well, half my life is great?" Why must we constantly give in to the negatives? Realistically, no matter how your perceive the glass, you are still left with the exact same amount of water, but having a positive outlook on the glass will bring you more gratitude for what you *do* have (rather than focusing on what you are missing).

Negativity is obviously something that we have increasingly emphasized over the years. I mean, watch the 6 o'clock news and see how little media attention is given to positives. It's pretty unbelievable to think about. Murder this and corruption that. What ever happened to the brave firefighter who saved a kitten from a burning building? How is that not front page news? If I ever feel the need to hear the news I go to a website called goodnewsnetwork.com on which all of the stories are positive. It's comforting to see that good deeds are always happening, they just aren't getting the media attention they deserve. That helps shift my perception paradigm.

When I am perceiving things positively, it feels like nothing can bring me down. It's like I'm wearing an invincible suit of armour that negativity cannot break down. Now who wouldn't want to wear that all day? Ideally, every positive thing that happens in our life should validate how beautiful life is, and the negative things that happen should strengthen us, and teach us valuable lessons about life. Not to mention the positive things in life wouldn't feel as significant if every single day was perfect. Just as music wouldn't be heard if it weren't for the silence between notes, positivity cannot be recognized without negative interruptions.

Perception is the key *to happiness.*

We've all heard the expression, "Money can't buy you happiness," and while most of us have a hard time seeing how daily shopping sprees and custom cars couldn't get us closer to our ideal life — it is the truth! Let's take a look at the group of celebrities in this world who have checked into rehab, or admitted that they are extremely depressed, and they have more money than we could ever know what to do with. They literally have more money than they could ever spend in a lifetime, a wife straight out of the Victoria Secret catalogue, more cars than we have fingers, and an en suite bathroom bigger than our entire house. How could they be miserable?

The truth is, no tangible item or wonderful, loving partner will ever bring us true happiness. The only person, place or thing that can bring us happiness is ourselves! So regardless of what we fill our lives with, unless we can find happiness from within, there will be nothing to truly celebrate. Sure we may be happy on occasion, or seem content enough with life, but I'm talking *true* happiness. Like wake up in the morning, smell the roses, and piss excellence kind of happiness! That comes from within. And it all stems from your perception of your life, and all that is in it.

I grew up watching both my parents get divorced twice a piece, so I figured "I'll be happy when I find my husband and we have a perfect marriage that lasts a lifetime." So I went out into the world, feeling incomplete until I found this piece of the puzzle that I "knew" would bring me happiness.

Bam! Mr. Wonderful walked into my office one day, It was love at first sight, all the stars aligned, and we started dating. Life was so blissful, and all I could think about was marrying him. He proposes to me at centre ice of our local ice arena (I'm a hockey player so this is my Cinderella story!) with the most gigantic diamond I have ever seen. This was it, now I could be happy. Everything I told myself that needed to happen in order to be happy had happened. How exciting!

Except... Life seemed more miserable than ever because I literally had everything I had ever dreamt of and still didn't feel happy. I wasn't *just* unhappy, but I had everything I ever wanted *and* I was unhappy. This seemed worse to me at the time. And we fought about things sometimes. This was nothing like the movies. I thought true love was supposed to be easy and seamless and only ever enjoyable?

Can we see where my perception of what life "should be" got in the way of the impeccable joy I could have been feeling?

The word "should" should (*ha ha*) be thrown in the dumpster, along with all your old perceptions of how life should be. I'm not suggesting you throw out your standards for life, but rather than thinking about how life should be, why can't we just simply *feel* how life is and base our decisions and actions on that? This would be living in the moment at its finest.

I was blinded by my expectations, and completely missed the fact that I was with an amazing man who fulfilled every one of my basic human needs. He made me feel significant, secure, loved, and totally accepted. But I couldn't accept the fact that we argued on occasion. My therapist later explained that she worries more about relationships who never argue, because in most cases they aren't investing enough in the relationship and are simply co-existing.

So I was engaged to a beautiful man, depressed, and I realized that my depression had nothing to do with my current life situation. How extremely frustrating. But how could I fix it? My fiancée constantly told me that I focused on the negatives too much, but it seemed so natural and comfortable to do so. It didn't feel like a conscious decision I was making, it was more like a natural magnetic pull towards the negativity in my life. That pull felt as real to me as gravity feels as it pulls us down to the ground, and yet I did not choose to live my life lying on the floor because I had completely surrendered to gravity, now had I?

But at the time, it was simply the only way I knew how to live. I might be able to change to a more positive perception for a few days, but I would eventually fall back into my old negative patterns. Until the fateful spring when I contracted my most gruesome, and incredibly crucial, infection. All of a sudden I was able to experience and fully understand the power of perception.

That three week infection had a way of breaking me down and changing my behaviour, similar to a dog in obedience class. Whatever it was that made me resort to negative feelings and perceptions, possibly a fear of vulnerability (as I'll explore in the next chapter), was broken down with physical weakness, and I saw that the only option I had in that dire time was to be positive. I had to rethink the entire situation with a more positive outlook. There was nothing else left to do. And that is why I'm so incredibly thankful for that experience, because I learned so much from it, and felt physically forced to do what I needed to do to change emotionally. The physical weakness forced me to face my fear of vulnerability, and that allowed me to lower my guard.

I'm desperately hoping that you can learn from my past experiences, rather than needing to go through health woes of your own to get you there in your own journey.

I want you to consciously force yourself into submission to try something new. Try to be positive, and allow yourself the time to learn. Believe it or not, it was my perception of how it "should" be that stopped me from making the positive changes I so desperately wanted. Isn't it ironic that I wanted so badly to change, but the issue I needed to change was stopping me from making the changes?

A perfect example of this behaviour was my introduction to meditation. I wanted to become more balanced, so I read a bunch of books on meditation and gave it a try. For any of you out there who deal with ADD or ADHD, trying to slow your mind or 'not focus on anything' is hell on Earth. And it was a futile goal as far as I was concerned. I read that your mind should be blank, and you should try counting from 1 to 10 without thinking about anything. It went a little something like this:

One. Don't think about anythingggg
Two. Don't think about anythingggg
Three. I wonder what's for dinner? Sh★t!!
One. Don't think about anythinggg
Two. I like meditating --double sh★t!!
One. Don't think about anythinggg
Two. Oh screw it. I give up.

I felt so discouraged that I couldn't free my mind of thought, and felt that I was failing if I wasn't doing it this way that I researched.

I decided to attend a meditation seminar, and see if I could get some help developing these super-skills with instruction. And when I got there I was taught that there is no right way to meditate. There are many methods, and it's natural for random thoughts to pop into your head, and when they do simply excuse them and continue. Realizing that my perception was all wrong, I went home and tried again. And without that idea of what it "should" be like, I was able to really relax and find the peace I was seeking. Now I meditate often, and sometimes find my best ideas while letting my mind wander.

But a simple perception could have got in my way of finding this amazingly useful tool.

How many things in our life have not met our expectations, but could be giving us great joy anyway? If we simply change our perceptions from what things should be, to what they are (and how that makes us feel); our entire world could transform without actually changing a single thing in it. It's an inspiring notion isn't it?

The Gist Of It

A fulfilled life has little to do with what is within it, and has everything to do with the perception we have about our lives, the people and things in it, and what our idea of happiness and fulfillment is.

If your idea of happiness is having more money, how will you ever find true happiness? You could make more money, sure, but with your goal being "having *more* money," you'd never be satisfied. You'll always need more and will never reach that point where you can feel satisfied. You need a perception change.

If you can be grateful for the simple pleasures in life, you will feel true happiness. That is a fact. If you appreciate the simple fact that you get to wake up every morning, how could a traffic jam get you down? Literally, *every* day you spend six feet above ground, rather than six underground is a perfect day. Each day brings new surprises and opportunities. But it's recognizing this and really living a life full of gratitude that will bring you true happiness.

If we can appreciate every little thing that goes right in our day-to-day, we will be overwhelmed with joy, and the few insignificant things that go wrong will not have the power they once did on our mood. I recall reading stories from people who worked at the World Trade Center but survived 9/11 because they were late for work. Some slept in, others' cars broke down, etc. These were all things that went wrong in their morning, but saved their lives that day. With a new perception, whenever I feel stressed about things not going the way I expected them to I ask myself "Is there a reason this has happened? Maybe there is a lesson I need to learn."

See struggles as challenges, or tests if you will. The universe will always test you as you become stronger. You don't just make a decision to become more than you currently are, and make the change seamlessly, and then are never tested again. Life has a funny way of always putting obstacles in your path, and you can either see that as frustrating and give up, or you can think "Universe, do I *really* need to prove to you yet again how strong I've become? Okay, let's do this thing!" When you see obstacles as a test, you feel much more eager to tackle them, and feel that pride in victory. If you look at obstacles as the worst case scenario and wonder why this is always happening to you, you're going to dread it and feel overwhelmed. See how a shift in perception creates two completely different outcomes?

Hard work on something you dislike is called stress, *but hard work on something you love is called* passion.

Every negative emotion we experience is simply a signal that something in our day, or lives, need to change. We are either perceiving things in a way to produce these negative emotions to happen, or we are doing something (or *not* doing something) that could have avoided it. If we can begin to perceive negative emotions this way, imagine the changes we can create in our lives.

Let's pretend I'm feeling extremely disappointed because I spent an hour getting ready for a dinner date, and my husband doesn't even seem to notice. It makes me feel insignificant and unloved. Did my husband's actions mean he doesn't love me? Perhaps he's distracted with something from work, or he's male and just doesn't notice things like us females do. My feelings are hurt because my husband didn't meet my expectations, simply put.

So I have two options in this situation:

I can either change my perception of the situation and think of the facts: he's male, he might be preoccupied with something else and hasn't noticed, or maybe he did notice and didn't communicate it effectively to me. Maybe I am putting expectations on him that he can never meet? But realistically I know he does love me, and I am not insignificant to him or he wouldn't be taking me out to my favourite restaurant for a date night. So I better switch gears and be a more pleasant date, rather than giving him death stares over our appetizers.

Or, I can change my procedures and communication. I can simply ask him if he likes my new dress, or the way I styled my hair, because most likely he does think I look beautiful. That might make me feel special. Or I can be vulnerable, and simply ask for what I need. How do you think my husband would react if I said "Honey, I spent an hour getting ready for our date because I really want you to know that I still care about how you view me, and I would really appreciate a compliment on how beautiful I look?" Or if I simply said "Could you just hug me for a few minutes before dinner? I really just need to feel your love in this moment." Who in their right mind wouldn't react sympathetically to this request? It isn't argumentative, and you will receive exactly what you want so desperately.

Is this not a more favourable outcome than ruining your entire date night because you're disappointed he didn't notice you got new highlights in your hair? Seriously.

Let's change our perception, and adjust our initiative to become more proactive, rather than reactive. If we feel something unfavourable, stop and analyze the feeling. Can we change the way we are viewing this? If not, can we communicate how we are feeling to our partner, friend, or co-worker? Surely there is some way to relieve this pressure without resorting to more pain, or a conflict. At first you'll still feel reactive and it may feel frustrating but this is a practise makes perfect situation, where the longer you work at it, the more natural it will become.

The Fix For It

Disappointment comes from your expectations not being met. The sooner you can realize this, and truly believe it, the closer you are to finding true happiness. Rather than looking at the things you don't have, be grateful for the things you do have. Imagine feeling appreciative all day, for all of the little things in life; think of the mood you would be in. That mood is literally a choice that we have to make daily.

We can make the decision to be thankful for all the positives in our life, or we can focus on the things we are lacking in our life. Glass half full or half empty? That is the question you must ask yourself all day, every day.

Perception is the one ingredient required for happiness. Nothing else matters.

You can be the happiest person alive with absolutely nothing at all, and you can also be the most miserable person with all the abundance in the world. And wherever you land on that spectrum, you have the same choice as the person standing next to you. That's the thing about true happiness, it's for everyone. We all get 24 hours in a day, and we all have the same opportunity for happiness. Every choice we make either brings us more or less happiness throughout the day.

If your car breaks down, you can choose to feel inconvenienced, or you can feel appreciative that the entire car didn't blow up, surely that would be worse than an alternator failing? If your car did blow up, be thankful you weren't in the car. If you were in the car, be thankful you're alive. No matter how grim the circumstances, there is always a silver lining, it's just whether or not you want to focus on that silver lining. If you do, you'll feel happy. If you don't, you'll feel less happy; it's that simple!

Changing your perception is not as easy as flipping a switch.. Well I guess it *is* that easy, but maintaining it requires some practise. No matter how great your intentions are at first, negativity will creep into your mind space. And just like my original perception of meditation, when a negative thought crosses your mind, don't overanalyse it or even recognize it, just dismiss it and move on. Having a negative thought distract you doesn't mean you've failed at changing your perception, it's simply a minor road block, and a great exercise to strengthen that positivity of yours!

I am by no means suggesting that I am this perfect balanced warrior who is peaceful and happy every minute. My entire life I have been a moody, reactive person, so I am not going to blow smoke up your *ss and tell you that I never succumb to my emotions. The difference now, though, is that I do not accept those emotions into my life any more. When I feel a strong negative feeling coming on I try to stop it before it grows too big. I try to slay the monster while it is still small. The idea is to shut down the negativity when it's at a 1-2, rather than controlling it when you're nearing a 10.

I control the growth of my inner Hulk by questioning the emotions. I am constantly quizzing myself on what's important, and reminding myself that feeling that emotional balance is more important than reacting to something petty. Acceptance of the current situation is what having a positive perception is all about.

I read a wonderful analogy of how you should treat negativity, because in most cases that negativity shows up like an angry customer at a customer service desk. A part of you is dissatisfied with the situation, and needs to make you aware of the situation, and from there we react. If you return the complaint with rudeness, the angry customer will get more upset and more unruly. If you politely explain that right now you are busy, but you'd be happy to help them at your next convenience; they will be much more understanding and hopefully wait their turn.

When we react immediately on an negative emotion or feeling, the results can be extreme. But if we dismiss the issue all together, that can frustrate us as well because our concerns aren't being dealt with. So if we can calmly say "I can't deal with this right now, but will at my earliest convenience," you can finish what you are doing, keep your positivity in check, and if the frustration doesn't wear off in that time you've been preoccupied, then you can revisit it with a clear mind and come up with a solution for the issue. Perhaps you need to communicate with someone, or prepare in the future to avoid another situation like the one you just experienced.

Only you can change your perception. You can't wait for the time to be right. When you're up sh*t creek without a paddle, that's the best time of all to change your perception, because you can see how much of an impact this decision can make.

There's no smoke and mirrors, no tricks of the trade on this one. Make the decision to see that glass as half full, all day and all night. At first it will feel forced, and by all means it will be. You might not completely commit to it to start, but like a weak muscle in the gym, the more you practise and work that muscle out, the stronger it naturally becomes. Before you know it, you realize you're not reacting to things that used to get you fired up. That gives you confidence, and when you get a hold of confidence there isn't a thing on this planet you can't achieve!

Push forward with a positive perception and everything you wished for in life will eventually be yours.

Nothing in particular has to change in your life, just your perception, and then everything can change in your life.

Abraham Lincoln said "Most folks are about as happy as they want to be." So how happy do *you* want to be? That is the question. Try it now, and see for yourself!

Accepting Vulnerability

Vulnerability is my emotional Achilles' heel. It is my weakest point, and one that I need most for balance. It took me the longest to recognize this issue and it is an ongoing struggle to remain comfortable while feeling vulnerable.

During my childhood I developed an innate ability to avoid vulnerability, because in the circumstances I found myself in I needed to appear strong. I felt like I had played the victim for long enough, and vowed to not feel that way again. I wanted to be the hunter and never the hunted. Vulnerability meant I was available to be hurt, and by avoiding it I felt like I could avoid pain. But unfortunately, this simply delayed the inevitable until I recognized how badly my lack of vulnerability was affecting not only my ability to feel regular necessary emotions, but was also negatively affecting my relationships.

I was quick to act out in anger whenever undesirable emotions were felt, and I reacted like an insecure dog who barks to hide their own fears and worries of the current situation. Writing this book has brought a whole new level of vulnerability into my life. Not only am I exposing my life, my heart and my soul into these pages, but people I know well, and also have never met, will all be welcome to explore and critique my work on a broad scale. This book's release is essentially a major test for my new-found comfort with vulnerability!

So what is it about vulnerability that causes such fear in our society? I believe there are many reasons, but one of the biggest would be the perception that vulnerability is weakness. When you are vulnerable you are opening your heart to all of life's meaningful experiences, good and bad. So when something great happens while you are vulnerable, you will feel immense joy at the core of your being. But if something negative occurs, there is potential for some deep pain without that guarded demeanour that many of us carry around for protection.

That potential, whether it has happened in your past or not, can often subconsciously teach us to avoid vulnerability. We all live our lives yearning to avoid pain and seek pleasure. This is true with everything that we do, but unfortunately these two basic human needs can seem counter-productive to one another.

A perfect example is our need for connection. Humans are one of the few species on the planet who actually require emotional connection to survive. There was research done many years ago in orphanages, because there was a mortality rate in infants up to 40%, and they found that regardless of proper nutrition, if a baby was not held and nuzzled enough, it would physically stop growing, and would in time, die. The need for human connection is so essential that we can actually die from not experiencing it.

But the ability to truly connect on a profound level requires a certain amount of vulnerability. So if we have a fear of vulnerability, and it impedes our ability to make meaningful relationships, then we are starving ourselves of an essential ingredient for a fulfilled life. And that negative feeling could create an even larger issue with vulnerability because now you are jaded and resentful of your lack of meaningful relationships. And the pattern continues.

So if the feeling of vulnerability equates to pain, but lack of human connection also feels like pain — how do we fix the issue, avoid pain, and gain pleasure?

The answer is first to identify the issue. For the vast majority of my life, I did not realize I had an issue with vulnerability. Sure I was a tomboy and an athlete, so I acted pretty macho to fit in with my male teammates. I followed that pattern my entire life; I believed I was being brave by following my own path, and being my own person. When in reality, vulnerability is our most accurate measure of courage, and being vulnerable is the ultimate display of your authentic self.

Think of people you know whom you admire. Do you not appreciate speaking with someone who is very genuine and authentic? It leaves this lasting impression long after the conversation is over, and it makes that person so much more intriguing. Unfortunately this is a bit of a lost art, and most people assume roles in which they think are fitting, or more appropriate to attract the most potential connections. And that is exactly what I was guilty of doing all those years. I felt like if I was "one of the guys" that this would mean more meaningful relationships and a sense of belonging, but the issue is, that isn't who my authentic self was. So I was expending a lot of energy playing the role of who I thought I should be, and never took the time to identify who I was at the core of my being. I had no sense of self-awareness to even identify who my authentic self was at the time.

Identifying your authentic self is critically important, and is something that requires vast research and a lot of invested hours. But to find confidence in this true self once it's discovered (without all the frills and gimmicks), that is quite another battle. I began to realize that my larger than life persona was not who I wanted to be any longer, and that it had been a cover up for my insecurities all along. But I was stumped on how to make the adjustments to better represent myself as an individual.

After all, people had come to expect a certain behaviour of me and if I wasn't that person anymore they could be disappointed and perhaps even turned off. I could potentially lose friends that I had known for years, because they had only known an unauthentic version of me. This was the beginning of my path to vulnerability.

It was accepting that I am who I am, and if someone didn't like it, then they clearly weren't destined to be my friend for the long haul. And while that thought seemed painful at the time, the idea that I could find people who would accept my authentic, vulnerable self was very intriguing as well. Thinking that I could meet up with friends and be 100% my true self, without conforming into what would best accommodate others was inspiring.

The remedy for fear of vulnerability is knowing your true self, and finding the confidence to express yourself in an authentic way. Vulnerability is not something that needs to be feared, it is opening your heart to all of the pains and pleasures of your journey so that you can experience it in its entirety. If you are closing off parts of yourself to spare yourself some pain, I guarantee you are also closing yourself off to equal parts of pleasure.

Your heart is a highway for emotions, and if you close the entrance nothing can enter, not pain or pleasure. It's kind of an all or nothing kind of deal, here. If you want to experience the good, you will need to endure some pain as well. But it is having the confidence in yourself to know that no matter how much pain you're forced to endure, you must know with conviction that you can handle it. Many of us wear invisible body armour to help us from feeling vulnerable, but when we have the confidence to know we no longer need that armour, we can take it off and experience life the way it was meant to be experienced.

Often this armour is donned at a very young age subconsciously, as a method to survive stressful situations and the pressures of growing up. The recognition of this is very powerful because you can go back to that time, acknowledge that your young self was trying to protect you because you weren't strong enough at that point in time. Recognize that we are much stronger now, and we do not need to live in fear any longer. Take off that amour, and march gallantly into your future knowing that every emotion, good or bad, is meant to occur to teach you lessons along your journey.

And as an added safety net, surround yourself with people who support you in times of need. When you love with all your heart, people will line up to be a part of that experience. Genuine, authentic love is a gift that keeps on giving. You will attract the relationships you've always desired, and you will inspire others to love in the way that you love them. And you will have the opportunity to return the favour one day and assist when your friends are in need.

That is what human connection is all about. Opening your heart to others, and allowing them to open their hearts to you. There are no expectations or requirements for connection beyond keeping an open heart, and an open mind, to the idea that vulnerability is one of the greatest gifts you can give yourself and those around you.

It will feel odd at first, and potentially terrifying, but give it time. You may fall back into old patterns, and that's okay too. Just recognize your current behaviour, how it is negatively affecting your life, and remind yourself that you are strong enough to take on this world without that body armour. Take it off again, and step back into your life with confidence that you are being much more brave this way, with the acceptance of vulnerability.

The lows you experience (and survive!) will validate your strength and ability to endure, and the highs will be unlike anything you've ever experienced. That is because these feelings of joy and fulfillment will be unaffected by filters that you had placed on your heart to try and protect yourself from the world.

Life is to be lived, so accept the full spectrum of life's experiences and emotions that occur throughout your life.

Vulnerability is a catalyst for a truly fulfilling life.

The Gist of It

Vulnerability is at the core of your heart, and represents your authentic self. Vulnerability is a part of the absolute best of version of yourself, the one who is accepting of love and is so incredibly attractive to everyone around you. Vulnerability is a magnet for love, because when someone has experienced this raw version of yourself they too will be open to vulnerability, and you both will benefit from that openness of heart.

Vulnerability is an invitation for love and meaningful relationships into your life. True connections cannot be established without it; it is an essential need for love to grow.

Being vulnerable is an act of valour and bravery, and not a sign of weakness. You are removing the invisible body armour that in the past you felt you needed for protection, and you are replacing this fear with fearlessness, and replacing resistance with an openness to experience love at it's true potential. There are always risks associated with allowing yourself to feel, but the positives far outweigh the potential negatives, so we cannot allow fear to limit our lives any longer. We must be strong and know that we deserve to enjoy life and love to its full potential.

The more vulnerability and love you give, the more you will receive. Authenticity is always appreciated, and will attract more abundance into your life than you can ever imagine. And the beauty of being authentic to your true self is, it will never feel like work acting that certain way, because it is who you were born to be. You will act naturally and it will eventually become very comfortable.

We were all born with default characteristics that make us unique and wonderful, but when we succumb to fear we begin to lose touch with our authentic self. We become hard-wired to believe that we must act, look and be a certain way to be loved, when in fact, we are loveable just as we were born! People who are genuine and vulnerable are easier to love than those who resist vulnerability and connection. Think of children: they are as loveable as human beings get. Why? Because they are vulnerable. They are genuine and completely accepting of love. They do not waste time hiding the fact that they need love, they simply ask for it — kind of inspiring, isn't it?

Adults tend to hide their needs, and ultimately their vulnerability, because they worry about how other people may interpret them. We fear that people will let us down, hurt our feelings, or act differently towards us if we share our rawest needs and desires, and this may prevent us from making the changes that will ultimately bring us true fulfillment in life.

We cannot become so reliant on other people's approval to validate our worth. Every person that has ever met you has an opinion of you, so why would we fear people's opinions? They are out of our control, and there are thousands of them floating around. If you feel something (or need something) share it with people! Be authentic and true to yourself and the people who think highly of you will do great in your life, and people who do not value genuine people are probably not the best life fit anyway!

This is why we must take ample time to discover ourselves in an open manner, without any predispositions on how we *should* be. We are who we are for a reason, and that reason is to serve our destiny, whatever that may be. It is necessary to identify who you are at your core, and to express that every day. Put all fear aside and know that whoever is meant to be in your life, will be. And those who leave were never meant to be there in the first place.

Your authentic self will eventually become instinctual to you, and you will be able to take pride in the connections you have made in your lifetime, because they will all love you for who you really are, not for the version of you that you thought would be most appealing. When you are confident in yourself and what you offer, you will be more comfortable being vulnerable. That includes being vulnerable to the environment, to people's opinions, and to the trials and tribulations that will inevitably pop up over the course of your lifetime.

Without vulnerability there is no true connections, true love, or true anything. Nothing can be true until you are true to yourself.

The Fix For It

First you must identify what vulnerability means to you. This will be a great indicator on where you stand on the topic. If you relate pain to it, you must redefine it as a positive experience, and as a gateway to true love and fulfillment in life. Regardless of what happens in your life, you will not be able to enjoy it in its entirety unless you have dropped down those protective walls and shown true vulnerability. Remember that while those walls may protect you from some pain, they also keep the exceptional positive feelings out of your life as well.

Once you have identified your association of vulnerability and changed your perception to make it a positive in your life, it will be a tool in growing more meaningful relationships and connections.

We must build our self-awareness.

To be vulnerable is to be your truest and most authentic self, but how can we achieve this if we do not have a clear idea of who we are at the core of our being? Anyone can transform their behaviours to fit into any clique or concept, but your true self will always remain present within. It's taking a look within and thinking about what you feel in different situations that you begin to put together the puzzle of *you*. Piece by piece you will figure it out, and begin to embrace the quirks and true emotions that make you unique and special. Your ethics and morals are a part of your authenticity, as are your likes and dislikes.

Much of my reflection went back to my childhood: what did I enjoy, how did I play, how did I interact, and basically who was I at my most vulnerable stage in life? Who was I before I become so influenced by society? Who was I before I learned about who I should be rather than what came naturally to me?

To discover your authentic self, reflect on who you were as a child, before you were socially influenced:

Name an activity you loved to do as a child: ______________________

What brought you joy as a child? ______________________

Name qualities you love about yourself: ______________________

____

____

____

Are these qualities you love authentic? ______________________

We must take this time for ourselves and think not only about who we were, but also who we aspire to be in the future. The purpose of this exercise is to become the best version of you, *for* you. Never change to please another person, because that change is unnatural and not authentic to your true self. You will never feel true satisfaction and love for yourself if you are acting the way someone else wants you to behave.

Behaving aggressively is not within our natural authentic state either. This behaviour is almost always adopted through challenging life events, where we feel being outwardly strong is the only option we have. But this masculine energy only covers up the hurt and frightened being underneath the puffed-up chest. I know this first hand, because this is how I had lived my life since I was a small child. But underneath it all I was a feminine creature who was seeking love and protection, from the depths of my core. This was incredibly uncomfortable to accept, because my masculine energy made me resist the idea of needing another person in my life, and I saw weakness in needing support. But the more I realized the truth, and the more acceptance I had for my needs, the easier it began to act more authentically. Today vulnerability and love flows freely from my heart, and I do not fear bringing feminine energy to my relationship, or to any situation. Life is not a competition in which you must always be in control, it's about love and having your needs met, and my avoidance for connection kept me from living a fulfilled life full of protection, support, and love. I was unable to recognize what my needs were when I was acting out of my authentic state, because my masculine energy made me resist vulnerability, and accepting vulnerability is what ultimately opened the door to the life of my dreams!

Making these life changing discoveries about yourself is the beginning of your transformation. Finding your authentic self is critical in making any life transformation, because if you are living a life that does not run parallel with your spiritual self, you will always meet resistance from the elements and from within. One of the challenges once you have got an idea of what your authentic self is like, is beginning to live life as you were intended to. We have all developed habits that we repeat on a daily basis, from emotional demeanours to physical habits. There are always habits that we aren't the biggest fans of. Think of smoking — how many people love the fact that they smoke? Not many, right? They all say they will quit "one day" but it's that daily ritual of doing it that makes it so challenging to quit. Similar habits form in our lives in the way that we behave, and many of these habits were developed to cope with certain emotions, discomforts, or insecurities (not unlike smoking).

Once we have developed a solid sense of understanding for who we truly are, we will be able to see the gaps between our behaviour, persona, and our authentic self. It is embracing our true selves and acting naturally in our skin that is the most difficult of transitions. It is an incredibly vulnerable path to follow. Accept that you are who you are for a reason, with a purpose. If other people do not approve or agree with your authentic self, then that is an issue with them, and not you.

You cannot waiver on your personality and authentic traits, because they are all a part of what makes you unique. Be brave and be bold, and follow the path that was laid out for you and you alone. People will always have opinions, or they may ask you "Are you okay? You seem different," and this should be an indicator that you are truly making change. Reward yourself for following through and find motivation in these inquiries.

The fix for lack of vulnerability and discomfort with the concept is exposure to vulnerability. It is going to feel uncomfortable for a while, but you will reap the benefits once you have made peace with the experience. One day it will hit you and you will hardly recognize yourself in the mirror. You will love and accept yourself fully, you will act authentically throughout your day, you'll take pride in your personal development, and you'll appreciate all of your connections to others.

Your life will be fulfilling and enjoyable because you'll be living life to your own standards and experiencing life on your own terms. That is vulnerable living and that is how you become truly happy within.

Building a Better Body

Your body is a direct reflection of your life and you as a person, so what is your body saying about you? If you are lazy, it will show; conversely if you are disciplined, it will show. If you don't like the way that last sentence made you feel when you read it, you're most likely not happy with your current body shape. You may even feel angry with me for my choice of words, rather than taking responsibility for your actions (or lack thereof) resulting in your current health situation.

Our society has become plagued with heart disease, cancer, and obesity, and the media keeps preaching these "love thyself" and "love your curves" messages to brainwash you. Don't get me wrong: curves are fine, but blocked arteries are not.

Regardless of what you say, the way you look affects the way you feel about yourself, and sometimes feel in general. Try this sometime: if you wake up (or after work) and you're just not feeling that good, do your hair and makeup and put on one of your favourite outfits. I bet your mood will begin to improve.

Simple examples like those prove that there is a definite body-mind connection, and not just to us tree-loving hippies, but it even makes sense scientifically! If our bodies haven't been fed the right foods, exercised, or rested that is going to cause stress within our bodies. And that stress is going to affect us mentally. This is a fact!

Think about after a big Thanksgiving dinner, when you are stuffed to the limits, can barely move, and all you want to do is sleep. Where's your motivation levels at this point in time? Non-existent right? This is because our bodies have just been bombarded with a mass quantity of food it now has to process, and so all of our body's resources and energy is focused on getting that second helping digested. This leaves no energy for anything else. The same things applies when we eat foods that are terrible for us. Man-made processed foods (with ingredients we can't even pronounce) put our bodies into a state of emergency. Our bodies were designed to eat natural organic foods, like the rest of the planet's animals. So when we eat these convenient mystery foods, our bodies can't identify what it is, or what to do with it and in most cases simply stores it as fat. That's a safe place to store it so that it doesn't hurt our body; it only hurts our feelings when we see our reflection in a mirror!

Artificial sweeteners are the perfect example. Yes, it may contain zero calories, but it is also not a real food. Real sugar is something that was refined from sugar cane or sugar beet. Refined foods are generally a bad idea, but at least sugar came from something our bodies were designed to eat. So when we put sugar in our bodies, our bodies have some idea how to process it. "I'll use it for energy," the body says, but then we sit on our butts all day and don't need as much energy as we are eating, so our body eventually stores it away as fat (unfortunate but true). So at least when you eat real sugar — which I still don't recommend — your body has the opportunity to burn it as energy only if you are burning sufficient calories with daily exercise. Our bodies transform artificial sweeteners into fat immediately because they cannot be used for energy. It's like putting a non-flammable mystery log into a fire: it won't burn!

After years and years of dieting, losing weight, and putting it back on (plus a few!) I finally realized the real secret of staying healthy: *eating real food*. It sounds ridiculous and too simple, but it is true. In order for our bodies to maintain a strong immune system, it needs vitamins and nutrients, and those all come from natural foods. Anything else is a waste of your time and health.

We have become so driven by food that temporarily pleases our senses that we have forgotten what food's primary functions are: to nurture and fuel our bodies.

We need to start thinking of our bodies as an amazingly rare sports car: it's the only one like it in the world. So if we had a one of a kind hot rod, would we cheap out and get the lowest grade fuel for it? Or would we splurge and make sure we are putting the top grade fuel in it and treating it the way it deserves to be treated? Probably the latter. And yet when it comes to our bodies, we go with the 'quick fix' of convenience meals. Or we go for instant gratification and eat what tastes good regardless of the effects it can have on our health. It doesn't make much sense, does it?

I believe most diseases that occur are completely avoidable, including cancer. Our immune system is so incredibly important and valuable to us, but it is constantly compromised due to poor health decisions. As a society, we have become so obsessed with germs and bacteria that we have anti-bacterial soaps and cleaners for every inch of our houses, but we rarely focus on strengthening our own immune systems. I'm not saying anti-bacterial soaps are wrong, I'm just suggesting we do a little inside job on ourselves too, so that (heaven forbid) a germ gets through to us, we have an immune system ready to fight potential colds and flus.

A healthy diet is one that consists of whole foods, which generally means foods with one ingredient. When grocery shopping I strive to purchase all whole foods, and if I am going outside of fresh produce and meats, I will try to purchase foods with as close to one ingredient as possible and never foods with more than five. I've received grief from people for always reading nutrition labels, but I personally find it appalling that more people don't read what they are about to eat. That really freaks me out, and yet it is common practise in today's society. Do you really know what you are eating? Do you even care to know what you are putting into your body?

Next time you're in the grocery store, take a minute to see what is in the products you regularly purchase. How many different names for sugar are there? How about modified products? Words you've never seen before and can't pronounce? Why are we eating these mystery foods and preservatives? Sure you might be saving a little time and money, but at what cost? Your body! And you only get one of those, unlike most sports cars, there are no leases or trade-ins in this life. You've got one body to take care of, and it's got to last you a lifetime. Do you see the severity of the situation now?

Modified corn starch is an absolute no-no. If you see it, put it back: you're going to see it everywhere. I was just like you once: couldn't be bothered to take the time or spend the extra dollar for the real food. I would say "fresh produce is a waste because it goes bad." Food is supposed to go bad! It's really weird that much of our food doesn't go bad for months. What in the hell is it doing in our bodies if it has a shelf life of 2+ months?

There are many frozen vegetable options that are awesome. They don't spoil, they are typically just as nutritious as fresh produce, and you just heat them up and serve. How does it get easier than this?

Then there are the refined foods. Here's a perfect example for your mind to grasp. There is a plant called a coca plant, and from this plant you can chew the leaves, or make a tea. Coca-Cola actually uses a leaf extract of this plant currently in its products. But if you take this plant and refine the hell out of it, you get cocaine. Cocaine is a pretty far cry from your beloved Coca-Cola. The extraction of the cocaine from the coca plant is a multi-step process and the result is something much stronger than the original product.

White sugar is like cocaine in that it has been refined to a point where it is much more potent than its original form. It tastes sweeter and does more damage within your body, because it is not a naturally developing product. It had to be stripped and strengthened chemically to be extracted. Sugar has been linked to all kinds of physical illnesses from liver damage to cancer. But I guess that's just like everything else right? So why should we overreact?

The food industry is a billion-dollar business, and alongside marketing there are many sneaky tactics that can lead you astray. Foods like sugar and the many other nutritionally empty foods we consume affect us in simple ways to increase food sales. When we are eating food that is nutritionally poor, we may eat a large portion, but our bodies are still yearning for the vitamins and minerals that we require to effectively operate. So soon after we are finished with that meal, our body will tell us that we are still hungry. That is because our bodies are being nutritionally starved. Yes, physically we have just eaten a meal two times too big, but nutritionally we are starving ourselves. This means our appetite will never be satisfied, because our nutritional needs are never satisfied. Why can't we just feed our body what it actually needs?

Well the truth is you can, and it's not as hard as you think. It's all about habits. If you habitually go to the grocery store and buy the same crap, you'll continue to look like crap, and feel like crap too. But if you make this change a must, and put an effort into changing that grocery list, you'll be shocked at how simple it is to change. It's as easy as reading labels and doing some research. Stick with natural foods, and let your body validate your decision for you.

Healthy foods are one thing, and portion sizes are quite another. I know I personally had this issue, with eating way more than I need to for my petite stature. It's another habit, and all it takes is to recognize that you're doing it and stop. You'll feel hungry for a while, but eventually your stomach will shrink back to a more reasonable size for your body and you won't feel the urge to eat that much ever again.

There are two ways of going about this diet change, similar to jumping into a pool. Everyone has their own preference, and reasons for doing it one way or the other.

You can jump in head first and make all the food changes and start living your life in the most healthy way possible today. I highly recommend this method because you will feel the immediate benefits and will receive instant gratification from your body on why you made this amazing life altering decision. Plus you won't have crap in your kitchen cupboards, so there will be less temptation to cheat.

If you are doubting yourself and looking for a more gradual way of making these positive changes, you can start by dipping your toes in the shallow end. Change one whole meal of your day from some God-awful deep fried mess, to a garden salad with lots and lots of vegetables. Be careful about shopping for "health" foods in grocery stores. They may have green checks, gold stars, and whatever other stickers to assure you how healthy they are when in reality they are not healthy, and the manufacturer has simply paid a premium for some doctor or group to approve its product.

Whichever your decision on how to improve your health, you must make it now and take action immediately. Do not allow this to go on another day! Your body deserves so much more than what it is receiving.

I've experienced this power of change since switching from a protein-heavy diet to a vegetarian one. With changing my entire diet to include nothing but clean fuel I literally feel like I have a new lease on life. I have more energy, I look better than ever, and my body is responding in ways I never could have dreamt of.

I have literally silenced almost all of my sugar cravings. This was a life-changing miracle for me. In the past, I was so addicted to sugar, and when I wasn't eating it, I yearned for it. I never knew when my willpower would break free and I would go into a doughnut eating frenzy. Okay, maybe I'm being a tad bit extreme, but I did feel that way when I was limiting my diet too much and cutting out major food groups like carbohydrates to burn fat! But lately, since my diet has been so incredibly clean (think of the exotic car fuel) I have lost my drive for sugar. When I see it now, all I think of is my blood-glucose levels skyrocketing and how horrible that will feel. I realize this sounds bizarre, and no one thought it was more bizarre than myself as I was experiencing it. It takes time and consistency but the longer you stick with clean, natural foods the more your body begins to crave these foods, because it associates that food with nutrition, and so subconsciously your body begins to direct your interest to these foods. Junk food becomes easier to avoid, and when the day comes that you decide to treat yourself you'll really enjoy that moment with your treat of choice. Or you might be like me, who decided to splurge on a piece of ice cream cake and ended up feeling awful afterwards, which simply makes me avoid the junk food even more today. I truly believe that when my body begins running efficiently, due to my healthy diet, the junk food I once loved now does much more harm than good, and my body lets me know about it.

When I began eating clean my body immediately gave me positive feedback and it made it so much easier to stick with my program. It also helps to understand the science behind those pesky sugar cravings, so that we can avoid temptation when the time arises. The reason that we crave sugars and carbs dates way back before grocery stores and our convenient lives we experience today. Way back when there were hunters and gatherers, feasts and famines. Carbohydrates and sugars are both great energy sources, and back when starvation was a serious threat to our lives, an abundance of energy sources would guarantee our survival. Because this energy was so important to our survival, our bodies would send us internal messages encouraging us to eat these foods. Back then, the more fat we could store on our bodies the better, because there would be famine coming each Winter (not unlike a bear hibernating needs to store fat to survive). Our bodies never did figure out that famine is no longer a real possibility for the majority of people in the Western world, so we still receive those encouraging internal messages from our bodies when we eat these high energy foods. The problem is that we continue to eat according to these feelings, without logically realizing that there will be no famine. We store lots of fat, do minimal physical activity and eat bigger portions than ever. As a society, we eat way more energy than we burn in a day, hence our obesity rates being so high. But when you begin eating nutritionally rich foods, your body will react in a new (and improved) way and will begin sending you those same encouraging internal messages that you once received from the carbs and sugars. These encouraging internal messages will be sent on behalf of your body finally being fed the nutrition it requires.

You can train your taste buds to crave healthier foods, and your cravings and tolerance for junk food will decrease. Once you adopt a healthier lifestyle, you begin to appreciate how good you feel, and the junk food that once haunted you is now simply something that will make you feel sluggish. That association is created over time, just as your positive association to junk food took you time to create as well. If this all sounds far-fetched, I understand completely. I never expected to enjoy fresh squeezed juices, salads, and avocado the way that I now do, but it's true! Your mind begins to take note to which foods brings it the most health benefits and you are rewarded with euphoria, similar to junk food without the awful hangover of guilt and fat to follow.

Our food intake is one of the most critically important things in our lives, and most of us do not put much thought or effort into it, which is why being overweight and unhealthy is an accepted part of growing older. But what if I told you it didn't have to be? Your immune system doesn't need to weaken, and you don't need to feel old as you age. I've read that you shouldn't let an old person move into your body. How can we avoid this? We begin with healthy eating, and not for a week or a month, but for life! You don't need to be perfect on your diet, but you need to ensure your body is getting all the essential nutrients it requires to remain healthy. If you need a treat, have it on top of all of the healthy calories you need to get into your day, and better yet squeeze in a workout around the time of this treat. Being healthy is all about being proactive rather than reactive, just like every other transformation in your life.

Eating clean has affected every part of my body: any acne I had has cleared up, my eyes seem to glow, and I just feel incredible in general. You don't realize the stress that a poor diet has on your overall health until you make a change and begin feeling the difference. Then you wonder how you ever survived feeling so lethargic and sluggish. In order to make these diet changes you must make the connection to food as fuel, and stop seeing food as a means of instant gratification or a way to cope with stress. Food fuels your body to complete the functions that are required to keep you alive, and if you're giving it low-grade fuel, you better expect that it's going to produce low-grade results. Since changing my diet I have felt an extreme change in my moods, emotional stability, physical energy, physical appearance, the list goes on and on.

I know we are all sick of hearing "It's not a diet, it's a lifestyle," but this truly is the fact at hand. You've got to give up the fad diets that last 30 days, because they are extreme, unhealthy, and temporary (as will be your results). We must begin to adopt new lifestyles that include regular exercise and a healthy diet full of vegetables and natural foods. I don't expect everyone reading this book to give up eating meat, but do incorporate more vegetables into your diet. I've read that vegetarians tend to be healthier not solely based on their giving up of meat products, but because of their increase in vegetable intake. You must learn to change your perceptions of food, focus on doing what is best for your health (not just your taste buds), and you must learn to begin cherishing nutrition the way you currently cherish junk food. Satisfaction is just as achievable while eating healthy foods, the difference is you don't hate yourself after eating a healthy meal.

When you begin to appreciate healthy foods for providing you with all the nutrients you require, and use mindful eating as a way to appreciate it, you begin to resent processed, unhealthy foods. Natural healthy foods are the ultimate remedy for whatever is ailing you!

Previous to my physical makeover of diet and exercise, I was being medicated for depression and ADHD. Both issues were extreme, and I couldn't see myself ever getting off of them. I believe I was on the medication for ADHD for about 3 years, and the depression medication for over 2 years. As soon as I began eating the healthiest, exercising often, and meditating daily, I felt less dependent on my medication. I ran out of my ADHD meds and figured I'd just try life without them (I have tried this in the past and drove my husband insane with my lack of concentration, and super-speed talking) and this time I was perfectly fine. Dropping the anti-depressants really intimidated me because like the ADHD medication, I had tried in the past and had felt pretty miserable. But allowing myself to run out yet again, I decided to go cold turkey. I'm not recommending this, as you normally would want to ease yourself off something so drastic (do as I say, not as I do). But I was able to move forward without them, and while the negative emotions coming back into my mind was uncomfortable, I was able to cope because I felt like my body had acquired an additional tolerance for stress.

It was then I realized how negatively my eating had been affecting my body. And at this time I was still eating relatively healthy compared to most, but I really noticed my body benefiting from the change to all whole foods, and (as a personal preference) vegetarian cuisine. It's been over a year now with absolutely no medication and I don't miss them one bit. I see the direct connection to physical and mental well-being. I hope you will find it too.

Now once you've hammered out a healthy eating regime, and adjusted those portion sizes, it's time to get active. Now I know that many people who are out of shape dread exercise. It's hard, time consuming, and embarrassing at times. But you will never get the results you're looking for, the body you desire, and the healthy benefits without putting in the work physically. I know making these commitments are scary, and I know we all fear failure, but the only way you can fail yourself at this point, is by neglecting your body and not committing to exercise. Fear is a perfectly natural reaction to going outside of our comfort zone, but you must recognize it and push through. Don't settle because you're afraid of failing. In my opinion, you've only ever truly failed if you don't try!

This life is a truly great one, and I don't know about you, but if I can get my body into its peak shape and prolong my life by 10, 20, heck maybe even 30 years, I'm going to do whatever it takes!

So where do we start? The thing about exercise is you need to have fun and you need variety. You may think that exercise isn't fun and that's that, but have you considered everything? What about swimming, or soccer, or squash? There are a million and one ways to get your heart rate up, and I'd be shocked if you hated every single one of those. If so, then you're going to need to find some urgency in your life and make this a priority. If your doctor told you tomorrow that your heart was failing and you needed to change your diet and begin strenuous exercise or you'll be dead in a week, you'd make it happen right? Well find that urgency now while you're still healthy! And you can add vitality and passion to your life, because your body and mind will feel so great.

I could write an entire book on fitness and health, but the most important thing here is to get moving. You don't need to go to the gym six days a week, but how about shooting for three? Anything to get that heart rate up and your body to start burning calories. I know that the more you go, and you start seeing results you're going to want to work out more often, and when you start clocking major hours in the gym you aren't as inclined to eat those treats in your office, because you know how hard you have been working on that dream body It's a beautiful thing when your body and mind start to work together for the greater good!

Your dream body can be whatever you desire, but first and foremost your dream body must be healthy. Avoiding exercise and clean eating will be your body's undoing, but there's good news: it's never too late to change your life. So let's start today!

The Gist of It

Progress will require absolute honesty to yourself, about yourself and it requires a level of authentic dissatisfaction in your current state. By constantly assuring yourself "It's not *that* bad," you are putting off action and will probably never begin the process. If you are honest with yourself, strip down naked, and take a good long look in the mirror at that body (even the parts you do NOT want to see) you'll get a pretty good indication on where you are at physically. Also be honest with yourself in terms of performance. Try and run up a flight of stairs, and take notes on how hard it was or how hard you are breathing. I'll never forget the day my husband laughed at me because I had run up a flight of stairs and was huffing and puffing. His laughter caused me to think about how out of shape I had become, and then it was time to get my buns back in my spandex, and back into that gym (spandex are optional here!).

Every person on this planet can improve, no matter how amazingly chiseled they may appear. No one is perfect, and that is something we must learn to embrace. Imperfection is simply an opportunity for improvement, and how exciting is that? Even if you set a goal, and you complete it, you'll probably think, "Well maybe I'll lose another ten pounds?" And that's the beauty of the human body; it is our ball of clay, to sculpt into whatever masterpiece we want, and the job is never done. There is always something that can be better, something we can perfect. It's an art, and not something to be stressed about.

Regardless of your current situation, you can mould your body into any shape or size you desire, it's just a matter of how much you're willing to sacrifice, and how disciplined you're willing to be. Don't make excuses, just be honest with yourself on where you currently are, and where you'd like to be.

One of the wonderful things about children is their ability to dream and hope for things. They don't think about what's not possible, or practical. They want something, and there is no question in their mind that they can achieve it. We must start thinking bigger in terms of our goals. Set a big whopper of a goal, break it into sub goals, and do not accept failure as an option. The only thing getting in the way of you and your dreams, is your reasoning on why you can't have them.

So make your goal, and pick one thing you can do *today* to take a step closer to achieving it. Throw out or donate all your junk food, rid your life of excuses and fears of failing, and burn those emergency fat pants! Do not accept failure, and it won't continue to plague you. This isn't going to be easy, but nothing in this life worth having is ever easy. There is no magical pill you can take that is going to get you your goals, so stop buying them.

Anything that tells you it'll make fat loss easy is either full of it or really bad for you physically. And the whole point of losing weight and getting fit is to become healthy. I'm so sick of people going to such unhealthy extremes to lose weight, and succeed but at the cost of the most important thing, your body! If you are not walking out of this endeavour better off physically, then I don't think it's worth your time.

Just because you can't see your internal organs doesn't mean you're not destroying them with your shortcuts. Get fit the healthy and natural way, or don't even bother. The natural way will take time, will be difficult and will require a lot of discipline, but will also leave you with results that last. We need to put faith in ourselves and know that we can make these changes, and we must learn to enjoy the process. We can become so outcome driven and wonder why we aren't "there" yet and it makes us want to give up, but we must understand that it took us years to get into the physical states that we are currently in, so results aren't going to show up in days. It will take as long as it takes, and it will also depend on how much effort you are putting in every day. If you are only putting in 50% effort, would you honestly expect results greater than that?

The only thing standing between you and your dream body are your excuses on why you can't achieve it. So let's accept this challenge, and give it all we've got! Believe me, if I can do this, anyone can do it. We must make changes today, and stop waiting for Monday. Monday will never come, change today and you'll be forced to gain momentum in your new direction!

The Fix For It

We must first identify what it is that we want, and be specific. Find pictures online or in magazines of what type of body you're looking for. Think of healthy improvements that you want to enjoy in your life (more energy, feeling sexier, etc). And make a list of the things you are currently feeling that you never want to feel again (that being healthier will help with fixing). Once we have a clear idea in our minds of what we truly desire, we have a starting point to our journey. We must use these motivators as fuel to really make a change. Make it a must to change, and you will find a way.

Write down some specific health and fitness goals below:

Ex. No cellulite on my legs ______________________

______________________ ______________________

______________________ ______________________

______________________ ______________________

What actions can you take to achieve the goals above?

E.g. Hire a personal trainer ______________________

______________________ ______________________

______________________ ______________________

______________________ ______________________

Write down why you *must* achieve these goals:

E.g. Extra years with my kids ______________________

______________________ ______________________

______________________ ______________________

______________________ ______________________

We are setting these goal for ourselves to become healthier, and so the specific motivation involved is important. There are so many decisions we must make in a day to choose the healthier alternatives, and once we have built up that willpower, nothing will get in your way. Not even the treats that once plagued you. Give yourself some time to eat clean, and when your body is really running better than ever and you feel confident enough to have a treat, you'll keep it within reason, so not to undo all your hard work. Or you might have a bit too much, and feel that familiar sluggish feeling again, and you won't want to do that again.

You must eat whole natural foods, and exercise regularly (with intensity) and you will see the results. *Results come when they are earned and not a moment sooner.* So if you're not seeing results, then you can bet your ass that you've either been cheating on your diet or not bringing enough intensity to your exercise. You can lie through your teeth to people about what you are doing to become healthy, but your body will never lie. It will always show you exactly how great you've been doing, and in some cases, how inconsistent you've been. What you eat in private, you wear in public!

Long term consistency always trumps short-term intensity
- Bruce Lee

Consistency is the most important thing when looking for real change. Every day you must focus on the task at hand, and eventually it will become simple and a way of life. I believe that life is to be enjoyed, so I'm not suggesting never having a treat again. But what I am proposing is to avoid those "impulse eats," such as those cookies that pop up in the office. You want to eat them for that instant gratification, and that's where you get in trouble, because those opportunities for sabotage will always come up.

What I have adopted is a planned cheat allowance. For example, if I know Christmas is coming up and I want to have a couple of cookies, I will plan for it. I know exactly how much I'll have and that it will be *worth* the extra calories. It is planned, so there isn't as much room for error, and it is a one-time deal. The anticipation makes the treat even more enjoyable because you've been dreaming of it for a few days. This practise also protects me from all the other opportunities that arise because I think "Nope, I'm having cookies on Christmas!" so the sacrifice of skipping that opportunity doesn't seem as extreme. I've built a hard rule that I don't eat treats unless they are planned. It takes the risk out of the equation, and I know the answer is no before the opportunity arises.

In the past I have been excellent at justifying treats, and it lead to the demise of many fitness goals. Now with hard rules burned into my mind, I am no longer in fear of temptation, because I already know the outcome for temptations to come, so there is no surprise. Preparedness is next to Godliness in the fitness world. Always have a healthy snack alternative for instant hunger pains, and always have an exit strategy out of dangerous situations where your goals could be compromised.

For me, diet has been about 80% of my fitness success; if my diet is spot on, the results will come. If my diet is inconsistent but I'm training very hard in the gym, I might see some results, but they will always be compromised by the softness of my body. Diet is so critical. There is simply no way around it!

In the gym, make sure your intensity is high and that you are focused on your goals. I see so many people taking really long breaks between sets, chit-chatting with their friends, and I also notice the same people never achieve results. When I walk into the gym, it's like

I am going to a job. I am not there to socialize or play around; I have a mission to accomplish and I want to get that job done in the least amount of time as possible. I don't want to spend three hours in the gym, doing the same amount of work I could do in an uninterrupted hour. The choice is yours, but the more seriously you take your time in the gym, the more results you will see. Have fun, but remain focused on what is important.

A trainer can often help with this, because there is a level of accountability, and your performance will have to meet expectations. But beware: there are a lot of trainers out there who are out to make a paycheque and not looking out for your best interest. Make sure you pick a reputable trainer, and make sure he or she is *fit*. I never understand why people would hire trainers that haven't at least achieved the body they are hoping for. If your trainer doesn't look as good or better than your dream body, you need a new trainer; they clearly have not figured it out themselves, and can't get you there either.

If you're looking for big changes in your body expect big changes to your habits to earn those results. There are no tricks or short cuts to make this transformation easier, it will require dedication, hard work, and consistency. Your training will need to be customized to your specific goals, because different body styles require different work to achieve them. If you're looking to lose fat, high intensity interval training, cardio, and weight training will be your best bet to burn as many calories as possible. If you're looking to build some muscle, get lifting weights. But do your research before lifting anything! There is nothing worse than spending hours in the gym, and getting no results because you don't know what you're doing. Personal trainers are expensive, but it might be worth buying a few introductory sessions to show you some of the basics if you're new to this. Or go for an online plan; many are free and break down workouts for each week. It doesn't get much simpler than that!

Women, it's so important that you don't fear lifting weights because you think it'll make you bulk up. The only thing in life that is ever going to make you bulk up is that cupcake you're indulging in at work! Weights are our friends, and will only help us burn more calories, because muscle burns 3x more calories per day than fat. So the more muscle you have on your body, the more calories your body naturally burns at a resting rate. And if you think about it, we all spend much more time in a day resting than at the gym, so why wouldn't you take advantage of that? Not to mention you can burn excess calories up to 48 hours after a solid weight training or HIIT (high intensity interval training) workout, rather than cardio where you're only burning calories during that cardio session. Do your homework, and get your butt in the gym!

The greatest mistake a man can make is to
sacrifice health for any other advantage.
-Arthur Schopenhauer

Make your overall health a priority, and when you begin to feel great I guarantee you'll begin to look great too! So stop looking for shortcuts, and get to work!

Achieving Goals

Who hasn't set a goal in their mind with full intentions of completing it, but after a few days/weeks/months of trying our "hardest" the results aren't coming and we give up? Think of an example quickly, or else I'll bring up your last New Year's resolution! Don't tempt me!

There are many reasons why our goals don't come to fruition, and I plan on explaining the process and giving you tools to apply for your goals in the future to make sure they are all fulfilled! It's all about three things: *structure, dedication, and accountability* to succeed. None of these things will cost you a dime, but they will benefit you your entire life!

Let's start evaluating these three factors, or lack thereof, starting with:

Obstacle #1: Lack of a Structured Game Plan

I don't know if you ever played the board game Monopoly in your lifetime, but if you did I'm sure we can all agree that game is so frustrating it can make you violently angry. No? Just me? Okay, well let's see where I'm going with this. My comparison here is your goals vs. Monopoly. Just like in the game of Monopoly, we all want to "win" in our goals — that is the ultimate happy ending we're all trying to achieve. And the frustration of playing this game is that most of us don't entirely understand the rules. And not understanding the rules, mixed with a long drawn out process (with limited results) can leave us all a little jaded. Are we starting to see the similarities between this game and our goals?

What I'm hinting at is that when we set our goals, we often do not recognize enough specifics, and this vague idea is a phantom that we can never truly achieve because we haven't clearly defined how to accomplish it, or even what our goal clearly looks like. For example, if our goal was to "make more money" how could we ever fulfill this fantasy? As mentioned earlier, we could make more money but once more money was made, our goal would still stand as "make more money" so we would have to make more. We are running on a hamster wheel with no hope of getting closer to our dreams! How frustrating! You never get to win. And that is a valid reason to quit playing for anyone.

We also tend to keep so many rules in life for how not to win, but have put little to no time thinking about clear guidelines for victory. We need to shift our focus from failure to victory and begin establishing custom life-winning game strategies in order to get our desired outcomes. Because focusing on all the ways you can fail is not only attracting that failure closer to you through the laws of attraction, but it is also distracting you from all the things you could be doing to obtain success.

We've all heard of setting SMART goals (specific, measurable, attainable, realistic, and time-bound goals) and I do believe in that concept of selecting your starting point. But what I feel is required to truly get a grasp of your goals are to dig deeper. Write down your

SMART goal and then ask, "What does that truly mean to me?" Think of how it will feel, what it will look like, what things you will do, what things you won't do, etc. Dive head over heels into this fantasy and enjoy a moment in that glory. Feel all of the excitement involved in your victory and envision the specifics of the outcome, most importantly the feelings that are produced. Indulge in the sweet satisfaction of completing your goal, and continue to savour that moment as a source of fuel in times when motivation is lacking.

It has been scientifically proven with athletes that when their mind actively simulates an exercise visually, their brain fires off signals to their body as though they are actually completing the exercise physically. Olympic athletes use this visualization method to prepare themselves for upcoming events, and I experienced this playing competitive hockey. It's real. So why couldn't we use our minds to simulate the ideal situation of our life, and fulfill all of the goals we so desperately want? And once you have felt that joy and satisfaction, it's going to make you want it even more. Just like watching a TV commercial makes you want whatever food is on the screen, this is going to make you crave the results you're setting out for. Mental imagery or visualization impacts you in every way: psychologically, emotionally, physically, technically, and tactically.

So now we have picked a SMART goal, visualized it being fulfilled, and we are motivated to make a change. What's next? We need a game plan on how we can execute this goal. How is it possible? Put the pen to paper and find out. Do *not* do this all in your mind, because it'll be too easy to forget, it's not enough effort spent, and you're holding yourself accountable by writing these ideas down. Begin by doing the following:

- Write down three SMART goals
- Brainstorm ideas for achieving goals
- Write ten reasons why you absolutely must have these goals (creating urgency and incentive)
- Write down your inventory of resources that can get you to your goals. (Strengths, tools, skills, friends, etc.)

- Research people who have successfully completed your goals and their methods

- Success doesn't happen by chance, it's a collection of daily habits that produce the results. If someone has what you want, become curious on how they achieved it, see what clues they have left behind, and then add those points to your brainstorming work.

I think we have officially found a starting point, correct? We have a list of potential game plans to achieve our goals, reasons why we want to accomplish them, and we've already tasted that sweet victory on our lips with visualization methods. Our goals are specific, have a time limit, and are measurable so we will know exactly when we've accomplished them. We are ready to go, and because you've invested all this time in the planning stages, you'll feel more equipped and obligated to get to action!

Now we pick our top brainstorming ideas, and simply select the first call to action. Then it's time to make a move; which brings us to our next challenge, finding the drive for action.

Obstacle #2: Lack of Drive and Dedication

What do you think comes first motivation or production? Most people would say motivation, because how else would you get started, right? WRONG! So many people wait around for this magical motivation to arrive and it never comes. We set a goal, and then wait. "I'm just not motivated right now," I used to say, but I had this mystifying faith that this enormous wave of motivation to do something would magically appear. It isn't coming. So stop waiting — and start doing!

Have you ever needed to clean the house, and dreaded the task passionately? Who hasn't? You saw a task that seemed like a lot to handle so you kept putting it off. But once you finally gave in and got started on one thing, you realized it wasn't as bad as you thought. It took half the time you anticipated, so you added one more task to your plan. Then another, then another. That's the thing about momentum, once you get started it's almost easier to keep going!

So if you have a goal, but no clear motivation to get started, stop waiting for this magical moment when the Mount Everest of dirty dishes is going to seem appealing, and just *do it*. Regardless of the goal or the task at hand, just do it and you'll be surprised to see that over time you'll gain momentum. Especially when you begin to recognize results.

If you don't feel motivated to work out, go to the gym for 15 minutes. I bet once you're there you'll begin to get into a different state and will end up working out for longer! If you have a bunch of e-mails to send, go send one. Once you're already in front of the computer I bet you'll send a few more out of the convenience of being in the right place to do so.

Whatever you do, just stop relying on motivation to get things done. Just get the work started and let momentum do the rest. I've lost track of the times I've started something I didn't want to do and immediately got hooked and ended up achieving much more than I initially intended to do. It was a struggle to make that first step, but after that it felt easier to keep going.

Drive is required to get started on your goal, and your dedication to the goal is what will keep you going when the times get tough. But how do we acquire either? Drive must be attained through frustration, frustration of what you currently have in conjunction with what you wish to have. If you feel content with what you have, what are the odds of you kicking your ass in gear and pushing it to the next level to achieve your dreams? Not very good, right, because we become too comfortable where we are. In order for real change to occur we have to make change an absolute must. We must create an urgency and passion within us, and we cannot allow failure as an option. Become dissatisfied with whatever is in conflict with your goal, and vow to change and never go back to the way things were.

We will never make serious improvements in our life without first recognizing that something needs to change, and now. Without accepting that something is simply not good enough for us, we will struggle to take those first steps in correcting the issue. I am suggesting that you get a little upset about the situation, so much so that you can't stand to bare it any longer, and it becomes an absolute must to change it.

Without that urgency, you're a dreamer wishing for a change in life rather than a doer who is going to do whatever it takes for a result that will bring you extreme satisfaction and self-worth. I'm not saying be dissatisfied with your life, but I am suggesting you pick something you want changed, and make it a *must* to change, for the sake of urgency and motivation.

Don't be afraid to get a little extreme! What's holding you back? Your intensity would obviously depend on the type of dream your striving for, as you don't need to listen to pump up jams to get as fired up to go grocery shopping if that was your lofty goal for the day. But I am also suggesting that there is *no* goal too big for you to accomplish.

Look on TV: I bet there's not a person on there who didn't have a dream just like you and I have. And the difference is that they didn't accept failure as an option, and they didn't stop pushing until their goal was met. Why are they so special? Do you really feel they have a superpower that us mere mortals cannot obtain? *Pffft*. Please! The world is at your fingertips, you just need to decide on what you want for yourself, and for the love of God, do not settle. On anything, ever. Life's too short to not follow your dreams!

Take that first step to your goal, and don't stop until you hit the finish line. This may include breaking your goal into sub-goals, which will help make the goal seem more achievable because we've all got to start somewhere. But whatever you do, no matter how small the first step — take it. Now!

So once we've got our game plan and start to work on this goal, do we expect to reap the benefits right away? Let's use the analogy of planting a garden. If we plant the seeds, and water our seedlings for a day, would we expect to return the next day and see a luscious garden to have grown? Of course not. Things take time. Delays do not mean denials, and we must keep reading those motivational lists we've made to keep ourselves motivated to follow through.

And what if in good time you're not seeing any results? Simply revisit your list of multiple potential options, and change your plans.

If you have tried something and it doesn't work out, it's not the end of the world; you have simply ruled out one option by process of elimination. Even if you swing and miss, you've still got plenty of strikes to spare! (I feel like I'm getting all my sports mixed up, ha ha. Are we playing baseball or bowling?) If you have a solid game plan with multiple options and plans, there is no need for fear of failure. If you fall down, get back up again, and again and again.

If you truly want something bad enough you will fight to get it, and the key to keeping your motivation and determination is your outlook on the situation. Just like it was explained in the 'Perception' chapter, you have the choice to believe that you are exactly where you are supposed to be in that particular moment. It is so easy to get discouraged and to stop believing what you want is achievable. But remember that it is also just as possible to push through with even more determination after you experience a setback. And that is what the difference is between a champ and a chump.

Where focus goes, energy flows — so focus on your gains and don't waste time or energy focusing on the negatives that are bound to show up in times of growth. Learn from the hard times, and use them as fuel to get through that first sub goal. Then you're onto the second. And before you know it you're done that one too. Don't forget to celebrate in the little victories. Every day I try to focus on "winning the day" and it's a perfect daily mantra to get you through your day. Your day is full of so many choices, and each step you take gets you closer to or further away from your goals. Make each step count and win the day. As soon as you start feeling progress, any lack of determination will be a thing of the past.

And if you hit plateaus where you feel your motivation lacking, retrace your steps back to the beginning, note your progress, and get back to the things that brought you success. Sometimes the closer we get to our goals, the more we can subconsciously sabotage ourselves, so it's in those times that you must recognize what action got you there in the first place, and get back to it as soon as possible. Right back on track you go, no harm no foul!

So we've set our goals, and started to make some progress, what is the last obstacle that we must face? This obstacle is especially sneaky and will stop your progress dead in its tracks if you do not identify it fast enough.

Obstacle #3: Lack of Honesty and Accountability

Honesty and accountability in the world of goal setting are your classic good guys, your Batman and Robin (dare I say). And that would leave lack of both qualities to be your villains, Joker and the Riddler, which you'll spend your lifetime trying to defeat.

Without these two integral pieces of the puzzle, long term success begins to fade in the darkness. Many of these goals are not something you can accomplish in one sitting, so you're in it for the long haul. Honesty and accountability are your tune-ups for your goal. Just as a vehicle needs to be inspected and all the fluids topped up, so your goal needs to be evaluated and adjusted from time to time to keep you on track.

Honesty at the very beginning of your goals is especially critical, because it will guide you and keep you motivated. I find there are two different biases that we can sometimes rely on to avoid the absolute truth: We *over*react or *under*react to a situation, rather than calling a spade a spade. Weight is an easy example that most people can relate to.

When we gain weight, there are two ways to avoid action: ignoring the issue and assuring ourselves "It's not that bad," and that we've only gained a little bit. This is dangerous because we are accepting something that we do not approve of, and with this sense of security we aren't going to kick it into high gear to fix the situation. We might also underestimate the negative effects of cheating on our diet or skipping the gym if we do not acknowledge the seriousness of the situation

Or the other extreme is to blow the issue out of proportion and make it appear impossible to change. "This is hopeless," you might say, or "It's just not possible for me." Realistically we all have this moment in time where we either commit to change, or we give up. Regardless of the reasons we give up, there is always a point where we could decide we are not going to stand for it anymore. We can stop throwing ourselves a pity party, and get pissed off to the point where we are making a change come hell or high water. Once you've found that inner fighter, cherish it and be aware if anything helped create it, such as a friend or a song. Then you can go back to that source if you ever feel your motivation lacking again in the future.

When we see we are gaining weight, we need to be honest with ourselves. Don't sugar coat it, and don't make it much worse than it is. Say "I am getting fat and I don't approve of this, so I am going to change it." It's that simple. That little dose of honesty will be enough to identify the issue, and get motivated to change.

Perception is so critical in these moments because being honest with yourself is a very difficult thing to do, and is very uncomfortable at first. This is something I've come to terms with while training for my very first fitness competition. In a perfect world, I'd appreciate only focusing on the positives and every day patting myself on the back for a job well done. But unfortunately, there are days when those pats on the back aren't deserved, and things I am doing must be changed if I'm going to accomplish my goals. When you are serious about a goal, you need to find balance between positivity and accountability.

Positive self-talk is such a great tool to keep your motivation up, but if you're not doing everything you need to be doing to succeed, it simply isn't enough to get you to the finish line. That is where absolute honesty with yourself comes in. I am currently in the process of evaluating myself daily and inspecting my body for physical changes (good and bad!) I must be honest with myself if a certain body area is lagging behind, because it means I've neglected something. This was very frustrating for me at first, because I felt like I was doing a great job, but my body wasn't reflecting that same idea. It was only when I realized my shortcomings that I could correct them and start seeing the results I truly was aspiring for, Being brutally honest with myself is how I held myself accountable for my actions. It's tough, but also necessary for growth.

Accountability is something that, for me, felt like such an extreme sacrifice at first. Because it is a *must*, and an absolute priority in goal-setting. Sometimes we try to protect ourselves by giving ourselves credit before it is due, we do this by comparing ourselves to others, or comparing ourselves to our own past. "Well I'm better than I used to be," was a favourite but disempowering statement for me. It made me feel better about the current situation, but can you see how that provided a false sense of security and job well done, when I may not have been even close to my full potential in my actions?

If we are ignoring honest mistakes we are making, we are not helping ourselves achieve our goals. If we are comparing ourselves to other people, we are not helping ourselves achieve our goals. If we are settling half way to our goals because it's easier, we are not helping ourselves achieve our goals.

The only way you can help yourself is by taking accountability for your actions, being 100% honest with yourself every single day, and by making sure you're following through.

Something I've recently adopted and am finding great success with is a daily morning ritual of writing. I've had to add something to the beginning of my day to remind me of my goals, and fill my morning with positivity before I start my day. So I wake up, and before my breakfast I write down the following (hand written, not typed — it's got to be personal).

1. What I am grateful for? (at least 3 things, and try to keep them different every day)

    » This reminds me first thing in the morning of what I'm grateful for, which helps me live with gratitude in my heart and feel appreciation for all the little things going right in my life

2. My goals (at least three):

    » I write these to remind myself daily of what I need to focus on. They can be as little or big as you want. This is you taking accountability daily for what you want to achieve and it's a great way to start your day with focus and motivation!

3. Why I want to achieve my goals (listed about):

    » This is for a little extra motivation to practise discipline in the goals I've set above. Because writing them down without connecting emotionally to the goals isn't going to give you that drive to succeed!

4. Daily affirmations (at least three):

- » Affirmations are always in the present tense, so write them as though you have already achieved your goals (ex. "I am an IFBB Bikini Pro and a Best-Selling author").
- » Feel free to get as crazy as you want, and you'll find in time that they begin to come true!

5. What I love about myself (at least three to five, shouldn't be hard, because you are AMAZING!):
    - » This is important so that we celebrate ourselves, and all the love we have for ourselves. It will boost self-worth and give you the confidence that you *can* achieve whatever goals you have set for your day.

This exercise only takes me 10-15 minutes, but it is invaluable to the production of my day. I have allotted a time slot for me to focus on my goals, and I do it specifically at the very beginning of my day so that I have stated my intentions for the day, and can move forward in achieving them throughout the day! This is the beginning of how I win the day!

There are many mental strategies that will assist you in achieving your goals, but you first must understand the power of your own thoughts. It's all about the laws of attraction, which states that "like attracts like." So if we are thinking about negative things happening, the universe will deliver them. If we visualize positive outcomes, the universe will deliver those as well. If you're stressed about bills, more bills will come. If you know with all of your heart that you will succeed, you absolutely will.

I remember watching a great interview with one of Hollywood's biggest stars. He had nothing to his name, and wanted so badly to be an actor. He would sit on the hills overlooking Hollywood every single day saying to himself, "This will be mine," and he actually wrote a cheque to himself for ten million dollars. Pretty bold right? He wrote the cheque and dated it for five years from that date. He set his specific goal of earning ten million dollars in five years and kept the cheque in his wallet.

He had complete faith that it would work out, and visualized how it would feel. He then proceeded to work his *ss off to achieve the goal. Because you can't just sit there, hoping for something, and doing absolutely nothing for it. There are no free rides! It was one week shy of five years when this actor landed a leading role in an amazing comedy, and he signed the contract for exactly ten million dollars! That is the true power of visualization and the power of your positive thinking.

I recommend beginning this journey of goal-setting and visualization by creating a "visualization board" where you paste pictures of all the things you truly desire on a piece of poster board, and hang it up somewhere that you will see it often. Use it to visualize all the things in your life and truly *feel* in your heart as though you already have them. And in time these things will begin to appear. To test this theory think about your own life, and think about anything that you have today that once was but a dream. A family, the perfect husband, a dream job, a dream car? Can you think of something? Many of those things we now take for granted, but I'm sure you can find something that you desired so desperately, that is now something you have! At the time that goal may have seemed impossible, but look at you now. Just because a dream seems lofty now, doesn't mean that in a few years you won't look back, with that goal achieved, and think of how it once seemed impossible too. Maybe you'll remember this book, and me saying so. I do love being right, so I hope you remember me! Maybe I should be manifesting that right now?

Another way to manifest your goals and dreams to fruition is to ensure that you are dreaming in present tense. If you have a goal set in the future, the universe will keep it in the future. If you say, "One day I hope to have (blank)," your dream will most likely stay in this faraway land and you will never reap the benefits. Set your goal, and strut around day to day like you've already got what you want. If you are driving around in a 1989 Acura Integra (my first car I'll have you know!), but wish you were driving a Ford GT, grip that steering wheel proudly as you drive down the road, and imagine what it would feel like. Envision the life you are living today *is* the life of your dreams. The more convincing you can make it, the more obvious it will be to the universe and the easier it will be to deliver to you. Don't wish that you have it, just have it. Fake it until you make it, I like to say!

This is an incredibly powerful tool to achieve your goals. You must set your goal, and have faith that it will happen. Have faith in yourself that you can achieve it, regardless of how difficult or lofty it may seem in that moment. We know now that perception is everything, and staying accountable and honest with yourself will keep you on track to achieve. If you have done everything in your power to achieve greatness, and you have remained positive and full of faith that you deserve this greatness, it is destined to come true.

The Gist of It

To achieve a goal, you must demand change. Change will only occur if you find the urgency to turn your wants into needs, and your shoulds into musts! Once you have found what you must change, you need to come up with a specific measurable goal and come up with multiple plans for action.

Take the time to pause time and really imagine what your goal will feel like when it's complete. Get a specific vision in your mind of what the completed goal will look like. Giving the result that much realism will keep you more driven to achieve it! Once you can connect the splendour of the dream to the hard work it will require, the more drive you will have to get started and stick with it.

Schedule specific action to occur daily, weekly, and monthly to keep yourself accountable. You must be absolutely honest with yourself on a daily basis to ensure you are doing everything in your power to achieve your goals. If something happens to impede your progress, you must decide to view that challenge as just that: a challenge!. When you make a goal an absolute must, you will do anything to achieve it, and won't accept no for an answer.

Your first step doesn't need to be massive, it just needs to be taken. Once you start with one task, it's easier to gain momentum and start with the next task. Momentum is one of the greatest tools to rely on. Telling yourself you'll wait for motivation is simply a form of procrastination. Motivation isn't something your fairy Godmother is going to magically grant you one day. It comes and goes, but you must push through your motivational highs and lows, and complete the tasks with or without it. Once you get started, and start seeing some results, you'll gain momentum, and that is one of the greatest conductors for motivation!

We all want that feeling of success, and so it is important to set sub goals within your goal, so that the job seems less daunting, and you have more opportunities to celebrate. Celebrating is important to keep your motivation up, but it is important to remain honest with yourself on the effort you are putting in. Rewarding a job well done when it hasn't fully be earned can be very counter-productive in achieving your goals. Rate your efforts, or find some way of measuring your results on a daily or weekly basis. The buddy system is a great way to stay obligated (for lack of better words) to stick with your goals as well.

I once had a buddy system with a friend and we were both sticking to a strict diet. I would get text messages all hours of the day when temptation arose. But having that person to answer to is sometimes enough to put down that doughnut.

Social media is another great tool for accountability. Because you do not want to proudly post a goal on Facebook, and then not achieve it. That would be embarrassing. So maybe throw it out there and even tell people to hold you accountable for it. There's no going back after a step like that! Post progress pictures, and let people be involved in your journey. Maybe it'll even help inspire someone else to chase their own dreams.

Setting a mandatory "goal session" first thing in the morning is a great way to review your goals, and start your day off on the right foot. You remind yourself of all the reasons you want to achieve this goal, and write down affirmations to boost your confidence that you can achieve your goals. Setting this time for yourself is a big commitment, and probably something very different for you, but I find that making that commitment makes it easier to commit to the little things for your goals the rest of the day. Practise makes perfect!

At the end of the day, goals are not only judged by the outcome, but rather what you learned and how you grew in the process of the outcome. It is important to appreciate the journey, and all the life lessons that come along with it. The outcome is important, but don't let it be your only focus. You are developing skills and discipline that you will use the rest of your life, for all kinds of goals to come. Get stronger every day and appreciate all the things you're learning along the way!

The Fix For It

1. Pick your goal.
   - » Make it a *must* to change it, get disturbed about what you want to change, and make it an absolute priority every day
   - » Brainstorm different options to achieve your goal, and get started. If one plan doesn't work, try the next. Eventually you'll find the right path.
2. Visualize & feel that goal being accomplished.
   - » Making it real will make it more exciting, and will increase your motivation.
3. Get motivated or just get moving.
   - » Stop waiting for motivation to appear, take your first step and let momentum increase over time (along with results).
4. Stay accountable and honest.
   - » Honesty is the map to success, without it you'll never get there!
   - » Stay accountable to yourself, to friends, and to social media to keep you on track!
5. Make Sub-Goals.
   - » And celebrate all the little victories along the way!
6. Stick with it.

» Delays are not denials, don't give up!

7. Laws of Attraction.

   » If you are positive, you will attract positivity into your life

   » Act as though you have already achieved your goal, and are as successful as possible and that success will come to you

8. Hard-work and Consistency.

   » These are the two fundamentals required for growth and change.

   » Do not allow your work ethic to go up and down, along with your momentum. It must remain constant regardless of the twists and turns within your journey.

   » Long-term consistency always trumps short-term intensity

Creating Fulfillment

Fulfillment: wouldn't that be something you could celebrate? I can tell you with certainty that I spent most of my life completely unaware that I was unfulfilled in life. My past had been "good enough." I had decent boyfriends, was moving forward in life, and had a good enough friend base to keep me emotionally stable.

My life used to be grey. Safe, cool, grey. Nothing to write home about, but nothing to complain about either.

Today my life is a friggin' rainbow of colours, like cans of funky neon paint being thrown against a bare white wall. Everything is where it should be and it's an absolute joy to wake up every morning.

But how did I make that switch? It all started with a self-help book, kind of like the one you're reading now.

The books I read gave me a few suggestions, but it took me about half a year to put ideas to action. There are certain things that every human needs to feel fulfilled, and then many additional factors that are exclusive to individuals that they must figure out on their own.

For me it was easier to purge than to do any self-improvement on myself at the beginning, how incredibly lazy of me. The first step that I took, to create an environment that fulfillment could grow, was cutting ties with negativity. Now I mean all kinds of things here. The first is *people*. You know the ones I'm talking about — they never have anything positive to say about life. They will be the ones that you might want positive reinforcement from the most, but every step you take towards your goal, they will insist to cut you down a notch. Maybe they bitch about things that have nothing to do with you, right down to the weather and town that you live. In the world of Facebook, it's very easy to set these people apart from regular society. If there were awards for Most Depressing Status of the Year, they very well might take the prize. Delete them.

If it's a person at work who is constantly bringing your positive energy down, create distance from them. Sometimes this takes communication. Similar to the resentment chapter, you will need to simply explain how they are negatively affecting you. They will either take the hint and change their tone around you, or they might take offence and stop talking to you all together. Either outcome accomplishes the same goal: one less creator of negativity in your life. Yes, your work relationships must be cordial and functional, and that's exactly what you'll be left with when these co-workers skip you on their daily rounds of gossiping.

This may seem like an extreme metaphor, but if you had a friend who was constantly trying to injure or kill your pet, you'd probably flip out. We love our pets and someone endangering them would be on our sh★t list, right? Well, why don't we love ourselves and appreciate our happiness enough to stand up for it the same way we would our pet's well-being? How is our happiness any less important to our lives?

For me, a part of this was why I had to deal with my dad and our relationship. It was bringing me stress and negative energy every time we communicated. So by dealing with that relationship I not only rid myself of a lot of unnecessary negativity, but now that our relationship is awesome, I have replaced the negativity with positivity. There is nothing better than that!

Now negativity can be present in many forms outside of human connection. What about food or smoking? Both are coping mechanisms that we regret after we are done enjoying them. Regret is not a feeling that one expects in a life of fulfillment. Being a slave to cravings is not living a fulfilled life, it is a total state of discontentment, because you'll always need more to be happy. You haven't found happiness within yourself yet, so you rely on these bad habits to bring you a change of state. If something stressful happens in our day, the only way we are confident that we can change our state of mind from a negative one to a positive one is through using vices such as drinking, smoking, or eating.

As we recall in the goal-setting chapter, there are certain steps and procedures that we can take to stop these habits. But just keep those bad habits in mind when cutting negativity. Maybe take a pause and think about a bad habit of yours and how it subconsciously may be stressing you out. Perhaps you hate smoking, and want to quit but don't think that you can. Well whether you believe you can, or believe you can't — you're right either way. I promise you if you don't believe you can quit smoking, you won't. And if you believe you *can*, then the habit is as good as done.

We must become aware of the things keeping us from fulfillment such as subconscious stress, and simple things right in front of us that we are completely oblivious to. Simple stresses like physical clutter in your life, like a disastrous coat closet, or kitchen drawer can be causing you stress. It is so funny, because it is a low-grade stress, but every time you see it you will feel that stress, whether you recognize it or not. So set a time in your schedule to clean out that coat closet, and get the damn thing organized, and then wait and see what happens the next time you open it. You'll subconsciously revert back to when it was filthy and will dread seeing the disaster, but alas — you open to see a perfectly placed shoe rack and coats hung in all their glory. You'll realize then how much stress it was causing you, because it is no longer around, but your anticipation reminded you of how it used to make you feel. Think about it: your eyes and brain are obviously linked, so if there is something visually cluttered or chaotic in your home, office, or car, it's going to bring that chaos to your state of mind. So that's an easy, small goal to accomplish to get towards a more balanced mind frame.

Okay, so we've gone over a few methods of purging in your life, to create an environment where life can be truly cherished. We've cut out negative people and habits that consume our lives with things left to be desired, and we can clean up some of the visual chaos in our day-to-day. Now what?

Now we have this beautiful blank canvas with all the potential in the world, and no person, habit, or thing to interfere with our mission for a fulfilling life. But how in the heck do we create this magical feeing? It seems a little overwhelming at first doesn't it? If this were easy, everyone would be perfectly fulfilled in their lives. The difference here is that you are a part of a minority in this world, a small group of people who *want* more out of life and are willing to work for it. The norm isn't going to cut it. I hope you can celebrate that simple fact right now, because you even picking up this book to improve the quality of your life is truly amazing and applaudable!

For me, I had spent so many of my years trying to please others, I didn't even know what a fulfilled life would look like. So I had to put my pen to paper. Take this time to write down a few ideas of what you see in your fulfilled life. What does your dream life look like? What would you do today if you knew you couldn't fail? What does happiness look like to you? Taking this time to reflect mentally and acknowledging the specifics in your dream life is the first step to living a life of fulfillment. Write a brief summary below to get you started below, but this is something that you should reflect on often. And add as much as you'd like in the future too:

____

____

____

I tried to think of activities at first. What are things I'd enjoy doing in this new, fulfilled life. I was stumped. Every activity I had ever pursued was to gain approval and validation from the people I valued. So I had to go old school. What were the things that brought me the most joy as a child?

Those were simple times; we weren't quite so complicated. It was all about the simple pleasures in life. And for me that was art. I loved to draw, colour and paint as a kid. Bingo! I went out to the art store immediately after recalling my love of art (yes, I had completely forgotten about it to be honest). I grabbed a big canvas, some paints, and an easel and got to work. I put that paint brush to the canvas and began to glow. My smile was so big that my husband mentioned that he had never seen me beaming the way I was in that moment. I found something that satisfied my authentic self. It was a part of me that was unaffected by the stresses of life, and I had been subconsciously yearning for to bring me satisfaction. Now every time I paint, I am completely consumed by it, and it's one of my greatest therapies on Earth. It is a way to express myself, and my work makes for great, inexpensive gifts (bonus!).

So take a minute to think about different hobbies that bring you absolute joy. This can't be on behalf of other people's wishes, I mean something that is 100% authentic *you*. Maybe you have a hobby you've kept since you were young but don't do it enough, or maybe you're like me who became so out of touch with themselves that you've completely forgotten what brought you joy in the first place. But I beg you. Take a few minutes and think about it. It's these moments that allow us to reconnect with ourselves, and it helps move us along in our journey to inner peace.

One of the basic human needs for fulfillment is variety, so whether or not you can think of an old hobby, do something different. If you can't think of anything you used to do, how about something you have always wanted to do? Join a team, pick up yoga, start up a walking club. Whatever you want! We need to continue moving and growing as individuals. If you're not growing, you're dying and we can't expect to do the exact same thing every single day and feel fulfilled. You get bored. That's natural, so let's change it up. Something as simple as changing up the walking trail you go to every day can bring you adventures and exploration that will help liven up your routine. Clean your house with some of your favourite music playing in the background and hit some high notes in the kitchen with the broom as your microphone. Who cares if people think you're crazy? When did having fun make you crazy? I think it's crazy to live a predictable life, without spontaneity.

So once we have opened up our minds to having fun and finding some variety, we need to practise appreciation. Living a life of gratitude is living a life of fulfillment. You could have everything in this world and still be miserable, because you compare yourself to Suzy down the road with a sweet new BMW. You compare yourself to people that have more than you, and that makes you and your life less desirable in your own mind.

As I told you at the beginning of the book, I was always focusing on the one negative thing in my life. I would have everything that I ever wished for, but if one thing was out of sorts, it was all I could think of. That negative focus discredited all of the great aspects of my life. *Where focus goes, energy flows* — so let's make an effort to focus on the positive aspects of life. I'm not saying ignore things that need improving, but put the majority of your focus into the positive things that are great in your life, and is that not going to improve your outlook on your life? Without changing a thing *in* your life, you can completely change the way you feel about it. Kind of magical isn't it? It's not easy at first to make this switch, but if you keep working at it, it will get more natural and more convincing.

We must learn to love and accept what is currently in our lives, and simply strive for more abundance. If we focus on the negatives, that is what we will attract into our lives. When I feel myself become stressed or bothered about something I try to repeat the following prayer:

God grant me the serenity
to accept the things I cannot change
The courage to change the things I can
And the wisdom to know the difference.

We waste so much time worrying about things when half the time the circumstance is out of our control, and the other half of the things we could control it, but we refuse to do the work required for change. How ironic. Or moronic. Probably both!

I use that prayer as a mantra when I'm feeling frustrated about something and it helps me ask myself the questions necessary to assess what action is required.

Is this in my control?
If not, accept it and move on
If so, what can I do about it?

At the end of the day most of the things we stress about aren't even relevant a year from now. So what's the point? We are wasting our lives away being stressed about things that don't truly matter. We tend to "major in minor things" in life, and we must refocus our attention to the people and things that truly matter. We must begin to focus on what we are grateful for in life.

I am grateful for being alive today.
It is my joy and pleasure to live another wonderful day.
- Louise Hay

If we can live each day in gratitude for the simple things that we take advantage of like our health, having a roof over our heads, and having food on our plate, how could we even entertain these silly stresses that aren't really important? Now as soon as I feel stresses I begin to interrogate them. Pick them apart a bit. 99% of my stresses are so trivial that I can laugh them off. And I always ask myself the question: *Will this matter a year from now?* If the answer is no, is it really worth my time? NO! Forget about it, or do whatever you have to do to settle the issue, and then move on a swiftly as possible.

Life is to be enjoyed. If you hate your job, get a new one. If you hate your spouse, leave. It's really simple isn't it? Sure doing those things require planning, hurt feelings, and stress, but what's more important than the quality of your life? If you can make your happiness a priority in your life, the possibilities are endless.

What's the point of having a crisp blank canvas, if you only get to paint with colours you hate? How will you ever love the finished product? Loosen the reins, find what you love, and just do whatever makes you happy! Why must life be more complicated than that?

The Gist of It

I can only speak for my own life, but there were people, habits and clutter standing in the way of me and my own happiness. This includes mental clutter of past stresses, hurts, and experiences that left me worse for wear. Once I took the time to face these issues head on, I began to feel weight lifted from my shoulders. One little stress at a time off of my list left me lighter on my feet, and more free to skip to my next adventure.

I took the time required to identify the issues at hand and had to give myself a healthy dose of honesty. Sometimes the hardest part is simply being honest with ourselves about the good and bad influences in our lives. Many times I didn't want to believe what I was uncovering, but with each person I distanced myself from, I would recognize that life seemed brighter without their negative influence. To some people this may sound like a selfish approach to life, but if you can't be selfish with your own happiness then what can you stand up for?

I had people inquire about why I was being distant, and I explained to them what I needed and what I simply couldn't live with any longer. If they really wanted to be a part of my life, they would have to respect my boundaries and needs. And I'm sure they had needs too, but if those needs involved bringing negativity into my life, when I required positivity at all costs, then that's just not a good match for either of us.

From releasing the negative we must learn to fully accept the positives in our daily lives. We must express appreciation throughout our day, and that is a habit that begins a life of fulfillment.

By expressing gratitude daily, you will be acknowledging all of the amazing things in your life. At first, this will feel forced but in time (with practise) this gratitude will flow naturally, as will your feelings of fulfillment.

Fulfillment isn't about having everything you want, it's about wanting everything that you currently have. Show love for your life in its current state and you will attract more positivity into it. We must love without limits and begin to see each day as a blessing, because that's exactly what it is. That is the secret to living a divine and fulfilling life.

When you have truly found satisfaction in the ordinary, you will begin to live an extraordinary life! When you have found happiness in the current situation, you can begin to think about what additions you would enjoy, and pursue those. Once you have explored internally for what a fulfilled life looks like to you, you can begin setting up goals to achieve them. The work you do will earn the results, but your faith in the results is what will bring them into your life. Work without faith will not achieve the results you are desiring. Always work with faith in the results and good intentions in your heart, for there are no limits to what you can achieve when you love the process and believe in the outcome.

The Fix for It

Once I had set the stage for success by eliminating negativity as much as possible, I began finding the little pieces of the positivity puzzle to add to my life. For me this was finding hobbies and interests that I had as a child, to reconnect with myself and find things that I truly loved, but had lost touch with.

Another strategy was finding variety in my life. Think of your life — if you flat line. you die. Same goes for a life without variety. Keeping life fresh makes life more fun, enjoyable and fulfilling. It's those little adventures that we used to enjoy when life was simpler that we still crave subconsciously as adults.

Try something new, and if you can involve some of your friends it'll be even better. Maybe even make a new friend? The possibilities are endless if you're willing to put in the effort.

No amount of friends, hobbies, or interests will satisfy you if you haven't set your state of mind to a grateful one. Living a life of gratitude is the only way to truly obtain fulfillment. You must be thankful for every meal, every morning you wake up in good health, and every experience, good or bad, that occurs in your life. Everything happens for a reason, and even those terrible days are an opportunity to experience something new and to learn a valuable lesson. Stop focusing on the things you have no control over, and if there are things you don't like but can change, act! Make your happiness a priority and give yourself every opportunity to enjoy each wonderful day that you're alive. Remember: *It's not about having everything you want, it's about wanting everything you have.* The sooner you can see this, the sooner you can feel true happiness.

Thanksgiving should happen much more often than once a year. This should be a daily offering you share with the world.

I am the crazy person in my car holding back my urge to pull out the middle finger, and instead uttering to myself "Thank *you* for making me a stronger, more patient woman, driver who just cut me off!"

Why not? Life's too short to be pissed about everything! Think of the joys you could be missing while being miserable.

I see stories on TV of people dying of terminal illnesses, and they have found more fulfillment in their lives than people in perfect health. We need to take notes from people like this: people who refuse to let life drag them down. Regardless of the circumstances in front of you, you have every opportunity to seize the happiness in your own life. It's just a matter of seeing that for yourself and going for it!

What's stopping you? A little speeding ticket in the mail?

Make your happiness a priority and do not accept anything less. Period!

A Hot Mess No More: My Breakthrough

This chapter reveals the rawest form of myself, because I had a major breakthrough while writing this book. I have been pushing myself to my absolute limits physically, mentally, and spiritually, and when I had this Earth-shattering breakthrough I knew it was the purpose of this book writing journey.

Regardless of how many issues we work through, there is always something to learn. I used to feel upset about this because I would feel like I had completed my mental 'work,' and at that point in time I should feel 'fixed.' The problem with that is our naturally occurring observational selection bias. The best way to explain this phenomenon is to ask you to think about when you buy a new car. It may be a car that you hadn't seen around town much, and so you're excited to be original, but as soon as you start driving around town with your new car you begin to see the car everywhere you go. The same is when a pregnant woman might start noticing how many pregnant women are around. Whatever the niche, you begin to increase your frequency of seeing things around you that relate to something relevant you just incorporated into your life. The real question is why? Do you think the frequency of people getting pregnant or buying your car has increased, or are we simply beginning to notice these occurrences because our minds have selectively picked this item out and is recognizing it as significant now? This is a rhetorical question, as the second is true. That or you have an unbelievable impact on society and then clearly it is you who has influenced these births and purchases. If so, I'm honoured such a figurehead would take the time to read my book!

So the concept with exploring your mental and spiritual well-being often is, like your car purchase, your mind begins to notice things you never noticed before. Whether it is negative emotions or memories of hurt. You will continue to dig deeper into your life and feelings, and it is something that will continue the rest of your life. You become so in-tune to your body that you begin to discover things throughout the day and begin to analyze why you are feeling a certain way. This is a never ending cycle to help you with your own self-discovery.

The sooner you can recognize this, and be happy to discover more about yourself, the better off you will be. It is not a burden, it is an opportunity to gain more strength and wisdom about yourself, your past, and the way you learned to deal with issues. Knowledge is power, so the more you learn, the more you have to work with in developing yourself to be the best version of you that you can be.

You're probably wondering how this all leads to my big breakthrough right? Allow me to connect the dots.

As described earlier in this book, I had a colourful childhood wherein I experienced many issues that influenced how I evolved as a human being. In writing this book, I've had an opportunity to really embrace all of these life events and analyze how they are affecting me today. Recognizing these current issues were easier because I had made that observational selection bias and whenever I felt a negative emotion, and I would analyze why I was feeling it, and try to dig into the issue trying to see if my reaction emotion was actually covering up a completely different one.

Anger was one of my personal favourite cover ups. I was always very quick to react with anger when really I was feeling hurt (or upset) and this was a default setting I had learned very early in my life. I had an incredibly hard time correcting this reaction. I knew that I had self-confidence issues, and had a very hard time "loving myself" consistently. I had put a real priority on self-love recently and this is where I realized my deepest issue. I could repeat how much I loved myself throughout the day, and see some results on the surface but the problem was much deeper within. I recognized progress, but in the heat of the moment, and if the ingredients were right, I would resort to that default anger and it seemed beyond my control.

This has been going on the majority of my life. My acting out anger began that day I described my reaction to my step-dad in grade 6. I was a young girl who was forced to take a masculine role as protector of her family. My mother was not strong enough at the time to protect us, so I felt obligated to pick up the slack. This was not a role I chose, but one that I had been given no choice but to fulfill. When I gained the courage to act out against my step father, the results were incredible. I never had to live in that home again and my mom moved my entire family to our own home. This validated how valuable my masculine role proved to be.

Because I had already adopted that protector role, it was only natural to continue in that direction. I had authority in my home, and my mother respected me too much for my age. I would give advice, help discipline my siblings, and had developed way to manipulate my mother to get what I wanted.

As I began to play hockey on an all-male team, my need for masculinity was increased even more. In order to fit in with a group of boys, you essentially must act like one. There was no nail polish, or feminine qualities allowed. And I learned that to be accepted, was to be masculine. This was subconsciously noted and I lived the rest of my life based on those principles.

Maintaining a "tough" image, I saw weakness in femininity. Crying was something I would avoid at all costs, and I would act as though I didn't care what anyone thought of me. Deep inside I was desperate for acceptance and yearning for a safe, protective love; one that I had yet to receive my entire life. At the time, I didn't realize it, but now upon reflection it is all too obvious.

By the time I was an young adult, I had acquired quite a reputation. I was playing semi-professional hockey, playing against women that I looked up to my entire life. I had always linked my accomplishments to my self-worth, so at this time I felt pretty positive with who I had become.

I had also developed my own alter-ego, *Pearl.*

Pearl (or "Black Pearl" as some referred to her) was a version of myself who rebelled and did as she pleased. As soon as I would start drinking, she would emerge. She was infamous for getting what she wanted, and for doing exactly what she wanted regardless of the outcome. She was known for such amusing behaviour as punching strangers off of dancing podiums because she felt they impeded on her personal space. Or who can forget the time she punched a metal parking meter, breaking her wrist in the process. She was, by all definitions, a hot mess.

She was the epitome of masculine. She wanted to have fun, and not be bothered with anything else. Confrontation always resulted in aggression or violence, sometimes both. She feared nothing, and thrived on feeling significant. She talked loud, loved to make people laugh (whether it was at her joke, or at her, it made no difference), and loved being one of the guys. She knew more about the National Hockey League than most men she'd meet, and that made her feel significant. She'd chew tobacco to raise an eyebrow. She would basically do anything to be different, and that rarely involved being feminine or classy. She was larger than life, and loved it that way.

As we age we begin to learn what is acceptable and what is not. Clearly Pearl landed in the unacceptable class, and so I began to reform and lessen my drinking. I began to realize that I do in fact care about what others think, and I was getting a little sick of always being the butt of a joke. But at the same time I felt like if I made fun of myself, then it would save me from anyone else possibly picking something out about me that wasn't favourable. It was a form of defence in a way, as I could pick myself apart before anyone else had the opportunity to.

I would laugh about Pearl, and blame things on her to avoid feeling uncomfortable for the actions that I did. But the older and more balanced I become, the more ashamed I would feel of those actions. And the more work I put into controlling my emotions, the more these little Pearl reactions would stick out in my memory. I wanted them gone. I was growing up and wasn't interested in that immature demeanour anymore, and I felt almost hostage to her grasp of my reactions.

I feared digging too deep into myself, because a part of me feared Pearl. She was a monster and I feared what might happen if we were to connect. I had felt all along that she was the Beast that caused all of my hurt and suffering. She was the reason I couldn't move forward in my life without dysfunction.

Yes I am talking about my alter-ego, but can you think of time that you acted out in a way that was *so* unlike you, that you almost felt like it was an entirely different person in that situation? Think of something you've done that you are ashamed of, or embarrassed of. Can you think of anything? Maybe it's just me...?

I wasn't consciously thinking of Pearl often, because honestly I had associated her more with my drunken endeavours than my sober mishaps. I just assumed I was a mess and had issues. But I hoped that one day I would love myself and would get past these issues.

Flash forward to New Year's Day, and I was busy with some mental recon. I'd been journaling every day for a while now, and trying to evaluate my feelings and associations to the past. Why they made me feel a certain way, how that feeling affects my actions, and how I can rewrite my story (like described in the 'Childhood' chapter). After an especially productive "dig" I felt the need to meditate.

As I explained earlier, meditation has been a wonderful tool for my growth, and is something I feel so passionately about. Doing it is to connect with yourself on the most spiritual level, and meet your authentic self in a sense that you cannot do without this experience. But when you get caught up in the conscious aspects of life, it is so easy to become distracted from the spiritual needs that we all have within.

On that day I felt some music may help me to slip deeper into my subconscious, and I began to search online for some nice relaxation meditation music. I had picked a relaxation meditation session online, when in the suggestions box I saw "Inner Child Connection Guided Meditation" and it stopped me in my tracks. I know my inner child and I have a colourful past, and I knew that I needed to connect with her, but until that moment I hadn't put enough effort into it. I had done work on the surface, and tried some visualization with my inner child, but nothing deep enough to really feel I had healed anything within.

This online recommendation was presented to me for a reason. I felt a pull towards the meditation, and I felt as though it was fate for it to show up on my screen. I changed my selection and began to listen to the guided meditation, cozy in my bed with just me, myself, and my ear buds.

This was a twenty minute guided meditation and was all about establishing the most important relationship that you will ever create in your life: the one between your conscious and subconscious minds. From the moment it began I became completely submersed in the meditation, it took me deeper within than I had ever gone. It began with understanding the conscious and subconscious mind, and he changed the terms from conscious and subconscious to the mother and inner child. Next I had to acknowledge my inner child, and feel her presence. I had to recognize that my inner child (or subconscious) was present within me, and to show appreciation for her presence in me.

It was a very raw, emotional experience and I instantly began to cry. Crying is still one of those things I'm getting used to because naturally I link crying to hurt or weakness, although I can now consciously recognize it as a sign of healing and a release of emotions.

I spent the next twenty minutes connecting to my inner child, and trying to establish trust between us. In an instant I realized so much: This infamous Pearl who I had demonized for the past ten years, wasn't a bad influence at all. She wasn't fearless, mean, or aggressive. She was that little girl who was afraid when I was young. The little girl who was fearful in her own home, and had no one to protect her. She acted out in anger because it was the only thing she knew, and she desperately needed love and protection.

I was overwhelmed with emotions. I could feel her hurt, suffering, and fear caused by the weight of the world on her shoulders, and complete abandonment from her mother: me. I had lived a painful childhood and vowed to feel as little pain as possible the rest of my life. Without ever dealing with my past wounds, and pains throughout my young life I would force any negative emotions to the back of my mind, or my subconscious (inner child) and would leave it there unresolved.

I avoided short term pain, by forcing long term pain within where it would haunt me until it was finally resolved. I had done to my subconscious what I felt my parents did to me: left me to deal with all the pain in the world alone, abandoned, and forced to protect myself. What a concept.

Once I identified my inner child as a separate internal being with feelings and needs of its own, it was an immediate call for action. I felt so much remorse for my actions, and needed to reconnect and make things right. I was guided to give a sincere apology for being neglectful and for not listening to the clues of that internal hurt. At this point in time I was in another world, visualizing this inner child standing physically in front of me, arms reached out to be held. I held her close, stroking her head, and in a tight embrace I whispered "I love you." And from the depths of my soul I meant it. I loved this inner child with every ounce of my being, and I knew that she needed me now more than ever. The past is the past, but I can protect this part of me for the rest of my life.

From that moment on, I knew I had to live my life with love for myself, and a feeling of sacred allegiance to my inner child. I truly realized in that moment that I am two people, within one body. My conscious mind makes all the surface decisions, but my subconscious is equally as important. It is my authentic self who is true to my moral compass, and basic human needs. She will guide me spiritually for the rest of my life, and in return I must protect her needs and ensure that she never feels alone again. I cannot ignore my feelings in any moment, because those emotions are clues to what action I must take at that time. I either need to change my perception of that event, or change the actions in which I'm taking. It was an incredibly powerful revelation.

By taking this time to truly connect to my subconscious I was able to develop a relationship based on love, acceptance and forgiveness, and in essence this meant learning to love myself, trust myself, and accept myself entirely for the woman that I am.

As we neared the end of this meditation, the perspective was switched from the mother to the inner child. I was completely overwhelmed. I felt every hurt emotion, abandonment, and fear burn in my eyes, and as tears streamed down my cheeks I felt the pain releasing from my body. I sobbed as the guide lead me through this emotional ride. I was the inner child being held by the mother, and the mother was acknowledging me and apologizing for being neglectful, just as I had done at the beginning of the meditation. I felt the warmth surround me, and the pain subsided. I recognized that I am no longer alone and abandoned, and that we will have each other to lean on for the rest of our lives. This feeling of love showering over me was so incredibly healing.

I soaked in that moment, and all that my inner child had yearned for had finally been delivered. She was not alone, she had been acknowledged, and above that, she had been loved unconditionally. I felt whole again for the first time in my memory.

As the meditation winded down, I was brought back into my conscious mind and instructed to open my eyes. As I slowly opened them, it was as if I was seeing the world for the first time. I was experiencing my life through new eyes, and I felt absolutely no pain inside. I wasn't always aware of the pain I felt inside subconsciously, but certainly noticed it missing in that moment. I felt free of the burdens and baggage I had been carrying around my entire life. I gently gave myself a hug, and with a megawatt smile I thought, "I love you," and I meant it. It was one of the most incredible moments of my life to date.

I felt like a brand new woman. Two women actually! I accepted that there will always be those two halves of my mind between my conscious and subconscious, and that this truly is the most important relationship I will ever have in my life. Now that this relationship has been introduced, it's a matter of establishing trust through action moving forward. I must learn to effectively recognize the emotions that I have always ignored, and eventually stored in my subconscious. If I am feeling reactive and falling back into my old habits, this is a sign that my inner child does not feel protected and is acting out, out of desperation. This is something I cannot have happen, because it means that I have abandon her again.

This will be a challenge to change the way I have always reacted to events, but if someone handed me a newborn baby and I knew I was the only chance this baby had at survival, I would make adjustments. Same concept for the health and well-being of my inner child. I am the one who controls how healthy and cared for my subconscious is, and it is solely my responsibility to ensure I protect her in our future so she can grow and develop naturally.

It has been nothing short of incredible to how this has transformed my every thought and action since my breakthrough. I am no longer weighed down with fear, because I feel stronger for having this relationship with myself. I know that no matter what happens in my life, I will never feel alone, because I have this relationship with the absolute core of myself. This is a relationship that is completely unaffected by anyone else on this planet. It is a love that is 100% mine, and it cannot be touched by another. It cannot be breached, and will be with me until the day I die. It is my responsibility, and my passion. It is my well-being.

By keeping this relationship strong, I know I can accomplish anything and everything I have ever dreamt of. When you feel this connection from within, you have no doubts of your own capabilities. Because you truly love yourself, and you know that between the two of you, you can work harder and persevere through any hard times that come your way.

Without fear, there is nothing that can stop you. With self-love anything is possible.

It wasn't until I shared this revelation with my husband that I was faced with one more breakthrough. This breakthrough brought it all full-circle and explained so much of my past. It was the last piece of the puzzle for me in that moment.

I told him about my meditation and the connection I had made with my Inner Child. Tears were building in my eyes, which is a very unfamiliar sight to my husband as it represents a raw and vulnerable side of me I usually prefer not to share. I explained how this subconscious mind, which I had always considered such a horrible monster, was actually this vulnerable scared little girl who only wanted to be loved. And his reply?

"She already has a name! She's been with you all along, but you always thought she was trouble."

I pondered for a moment trying to figure out what he was implying. And then it hit me — Pearl! I couldn't believe it was so. The drunken fits, the sober temper, the dark side of me that has been there my entire life, it was all her. But she was nothing like a Black Pearl, she was a wonderful, misunderstood beauty.

At the end of the day, my inner Beast is where I found my greatest inner Beauty.

My inner Pearl had been weathered from the elements, and dirtied up a lot. But it was time to see her for who she was, and it was time to shine her up back to her original beauty. Her beauty now radiates through me and is physically visible in all that I do. My eyes shine brighter, my posture is better, and I smile like a little child.

I have forgiven myself for all I have done, and I have let go of the painful memories that were causing me harm. Because our subconscious minds store most of our hurt and painful memories, they are also in control of keeping it in our mental inventory. When we can create a deep, trusting relationship with our subconscious mind we can suggest letting go of the hurt and the suffering. Once the pain is gone, you have a second chance at life.

The life of your dreams seems so attainable, and you feel so emotionally free to experience all the wonders in life. It truly is that simple. I have given myself another lease on life by creating the relationship of my dreams: with myself.

My subconscious mind did what it had to in times when support was scarce, and as I grew I was not strong enough to protect her the way I needed to. But now that I am in a secure place in my life, have the emotional strength and support system, and have the knowledge of what it takes to maintain this healthy relationship with myself; there is absolutely nothing that can stop me from fulfilling my destiny and living a life of love and abundance.

Since this breakthrough, I have continued my journey and have consistently explored self-help audio and books. Sometimes it is the simplest things that can bring the deepest impacts on your subconscious mind. Just last week I read the line "Are you fearful of being dominated like your mother was?" and in an instant my mind opened up to the key to my resistance to vulnerability. I still find it difficult to ask for help, and once I recognized that subconsciously I have been resisting any type of domination (such as help, guidance, or any other general helpful behaviours) I have been able to catch myself resisting and correcting my actions. This explains years of troubled relationships and my own stubbornness in many situations. It explains why I insist on never making mistakes, and why I always feel like I must know everything without assistance.

All stemming from a small child watching her mother in an abusive relationship and seeing her be dominated, I subconsciously made a decision in my mind that I would never put myself in a situation like that. But subconsciously that barrier created an overcompensation of resistance to dominance. In my younger years, I always had a love for watching male strippers, and had been very open about my enjoyment of degrading men. I couldn't explain why, but it made me feel good watching a grown man be in such a submissive, pleasing state. And now it is all too clear that I was enjoying the feeling of being the more dominant figure in the room, as that fit with my needs of never feeling dominated myself.

This lesson has been an amazing eye-opener and although it is incredibly simple, I could not have discovered it's life-changing message without reading that specific book and that particular sentence. With this new found knowledge I can ask myself questions relating to my fear of being dominated, and often I can recognize that I am overreacting (and that my husband lending a helping hand is in no way a form of domination).

The Gist of It

Self-exploration is the key for self-improvement. It is great to set personal growth goals and see them being accomplished one by one, but also realize that our work on this Earth will never be done. We will always be learning and growing, and finding more issues as we go. At the beginning of my personal growth journey, I found frustration in this because I felt like results should come and then the work is done. How naive I was in thinking that.

Truth be told, life would be terribly boring if we already learned everything we needed to know and then simply threw our lives in cruise control until we died. I have now come to appreciate the daily battles and lessons learned, because it reminds me of all the wonders that are included in this life. When I am learning, I feel alive. When I wipe-out and land on my face, I have learned to laugh at myself and then analyze what has occurred, so I can learn from my mistakes. I used to fear mistakes, but now I look forward to them. The universe has an unlimited source of lessons to teach us, but we miss so many of them because we become frustrated with different outcomes. One of life's greatest lessons is to learn to identify the lessons we are being taught in the first place.

In order to learn life's lessons, we must remain in the present. We must remain open and willing to receive the wisdom from the universe. And we absolutely must have faith in this life we are living. If we are doubting the process and feeling frustrated that something didn't turn out the way we planned, we are going to miss so much in this life.

We must realize that the universe has a much better plan for us, than we do. Always.

If something doesn't play out the way we planned, begin looking for reasons and lessons on the change of direction. Find the silver lining in every outcome, and thank the universe for always having your best interest in mind. Giving gratitude is one of the most important things you can do in your day to ensure your life changes for the best. Be forever grateful that you are alive on this day, and can be present for your next lesson to be learned. That is a wonderful gift you are receiving, and you might not even realize it.

When you feel you have nothing left to learn, ask the universe for guidance. Say "Please teach me what I need to learn so that I can grow," and "Please guide me so that I might be the highest form of self that I can be." I also like to give simple requests such as "If there is something I need to know or learn, please show me that lesson, I am ready to learn." There are any number of variations for these requests, and I welcome you to come up with some of your own. These requests begin to build your relationship with not only your spiritual self, but also with your creator and source of life here on Earth. Again, whoever you believe in, I don't judge! This spiritual connection is so valuable.

With the awareness that your personal growth journey is never over, and your spiritual awareness within, you will be destined to learn so many amazing things about yourself, and you can use this knowledge to be a much more effective version of yourself. When you have a deep understanding of who you are, and what you need in order to feel fulfilled, it is incredible what you can accomplish.

Just be sure to enjoy the journey. Have an outcome in mind, and follow your heart, and the specifics will unfold in whichever way they were intended to. Just have faith that you will become who you desire to be, and it will be.

The Fix For It

The fix for this is a simple one: Choose to be a greater version of yourself than you were yesterday. That is it.

Excellence is the sum of small, consistent positive changes you create and master throughout your day. The outcome of excellence will not happen overnight, but your own personal self-worth can rise starting this very second. You can become exactly who you wish to be this moment. Act like you are the very best version of yourself this moment. Walk like you are the very best version of yourself in this moment. Treat people like you are the very best version of yourself in this moment. It is but a choice to be the very best you can be, and although it will seem difficult to maintain initially, it will become second nature within time.

If you want to have more money, feel that you have more money right now. Imagine your car is your dream car and grip the steering wheel and smile ear to ear knowing exactly how it's going to feel. Walk around your office like you are the executive you wish to be one day, display that poise and confidence, and revel in the glory of feeling that success now, before you obtain it. The more we act out the behaviours and habits of the success we wish to attract, the more we will work to achieve this success.

Olympic athletes have been using this visualization technique for years to prepare for their sports. They envision every single step in their performance, and it prepares them for the real thing. Science has proven that they can actually stimulate the brain to feel as though they are actually physically completing the task they are imagining. Think of the last time you saw a really tasty treat, either on TV or in person, and without actually tasting it, your mouth began to water. Now, if you never tasted it, why was your mouth watering? It is because you have envisioned something that has sent a signal to your mind telling your mouth to water. If you took the time to truly imagine that same food in your mind, I bet you could make your own mouth water as well. Give it a try if you don't believe me!

So we all have an example of how our minds have been signalled to react to something we have seen or imagined, so why couldn't we condition our minds to truly feel and absorb the success and joy of having our dream car, job, and spouse today? We can make it feel as real as if we have it today, and that will fuel our fire to truly obtain this level of success in our lives.

This turn of events (bringing your life to the level that you desire) all begins with self-discovery, self-acceptance, and self-love. When you have all three of these self-awareness methods in action, there is absolutely nothing stopping you from achieving your goals! Never stop learning about yourself, and the things that you are passionate about. The more you know, the more you grow.

Change is a choice. Happiness is a choice. Action is a choice.

Make the right ones in a day and watch your life turn around completely.

Be bold, brave, and beautiful. I believe that you are already all three of these, so it is only you who needs convincing now.

Let's Recap

The ultimate goal in life is to establish a relationship within yourself, to which you can truly build self-love. This self-love will bring you unlimited happiness from within regardless of all of the external situations around you. There are people who have survived tremendous adversity and have been able to pick up the pieces and have lived fulfilled lives afterwards, and it is because of this connection from within, and love for themselves.

When you love yourself and have faith in who you are, there isn't a thing in this world that can take that from you. It makes you somewhat immune to the negativities and setbacks we all experience in this life.

Each hard time we face is simply a call to action and a lesson to be learned. When we have the confidence in ourselves to know that we can handle these adversities, all fear is pushed aside and life can be experienced fully in the moment.

We always begin with childhood issues, because they were the first influences on how we currently live our life. Very insignificant memories can make major changes on who you are today, and it is recognizing these memories that is the first step to your transformation. For me, I wanted to avoid all childhood memories, because I felt that they brought me pain in the moment, and by ignoring them I was promising pain in my future too. It wasn't until I could bravely face each and every specific situation that caused me pain that I was able to rewrite them on paper, and twist them with a more positive outlook. Things are never as bad as we recall them, and even if they are bad, they can always be worse. We obviously survived our pasts, or we wouldn't be here to complain about the pain we are experiencing. So there is always a silver lining, even in the darkest of clouds, and it is our duty to ourselves and our well-being to find these silver linings and to celebrate them.

By rewriting our past, we are changing our subconscious associations to those events, and with that comes freedom of pain and a deeper understanding of yourself. These are the building blocks of your new foundations. Without this first step, I never could have reached the point I am at in my life today. If you haven't already, please go back to the 'Childhood' chapter and complete the activities of identifying defining moments in your life (good and bad) and rewrite any events that need to be reflected in a more positive light. Remember that changing the story is not letting those in your life off the hook; it is simply allowing you off the hook for all of the pain that you are holding onto. Why punish yourself by holding those painful memories near your heart? Change them right now, and make a difference in your perspective!

Once you have identified the pains of your past, it is time to let go of the resentments that not only keep you shackled to your past, but also weigh you down subconsciously every single day in this present moment. Remember that resentment is like drinking poison and expecting the other person to die. It is a waste of your resources, and is something you must choose to let go. I couldn't have moved forward because I was anchored to my past hurts and hang ups, because I had never truly dealt with them. I knew how I felt about them, but never took the time to hold certain people accountable, and communicate with them to finally clear the air. This affected me every day because I was subconsciously stressed out about things I experienced years prior, so I had no "stress allowance" for any daily stresses that are inevitable in life.

I didn't want to feel like I was excusing their behaviour, and felt like holding onto those resentments was my way of punishing them when in reality they had no idea most of the time, and were busy living their lives unaffected. Forgiveness is not for the other person to feel better, it is for yourself to feel better. It is a wonderful gift of freedom from past hurt that is absolutely free, and emotionally priceless. All it takes is time, communication and a clear vision for what you want and need in your life. Clearly resentment isn't on that list of wants, so make the decision to leave it behind in the past, where it belongs. Forgive those who have hurt you in the past, if only for your own mental balance, and if anyone is currently mistreating you or not living up to your expectations, simply open the lines of communication. If they can't handle the fact that they are hurting you, or resent you for making requests that will require them to change a negative impact on your life, then maybe their friendship is worth reconsidering.

There are many people on this planet, and surely there are people who will fit in your life seamlessly, so it's just a matter of raising those standards, and never ever settling on anything in your life. Life is too short for bad relationships.

So why do we deal with bad relationships? The answer is fear. Fear is the reason we ever settle for anything in our lives. An acronym for fear is: False Events Appear Real. Can you see the accuracy in that acronym? We can conjure up scenarios in our minds that scare the living daylights out of us, but at the end of the day the only thing to fear is fear itself. Fear is the result of lack of faith, and an imaginative mind who creates horror stories in our lives.

Fear is nothing but a signal to prepare. When we feel fear about something it is either entirely false, and must be dismissed, or it is a call to action to prepare for something coming up in our lives. Our fear of public speaking indicates we must prepare and practise so that we can complete our task efficiently. And if we still feel fear after that, it is time to dismiss it. We have done all we can do with the topic, and now must leave that fear aside, and adopt faith that we *can* do it. No matter what the fear, know with all of your heart and spirit that you are strong enough to handle it. Don't waste another minute fearing something: Act on it and prepare, or cast it aside. Life is too short and precious to waste valuable minutes playing the "what if" game.

And if you insist on playing that game, really play it! Grab a pen and paper and write down your fears, then strip them down one by one. Okay what if this happened? Write an outcome. Then what would happen? Another outcome. Eventually you will come to the conclusion that you can handle it. The universe never gives you more than you can manage; you simply need to change your perception and associations of the situation and get to work. Work builds confidence, which will help you silence this doubtful voice in your mind raising more fears. Have faith and it will always work out! It may not end up exactly as you hoped or expected, but it will always work out. Work is still required, but work with faith that the outcome will be positive!

Having faith is the ultimate tool in succeeding in life. You must have faith within yourself to know that you can handle the tasks and challenges that are inevitable in your life. You must have faith in the universe and the path that it has put you on. Have faith in your destiny! You become what you think, so if you live your life constantly worrying (or praying for something bad to happen) you will attract all of these negative things that you fear. There is a law of attraction and you will manifest everything in your life with the thoughts that you repeat throughout the day, so whether they are negative or positive is entirely up to you.

Meditate, pray, go to church, or stay at home. Do yoga, or affirmations, maybe try both simultaneously? The important thing isn't *how* you find your inner peace, as long as you find it. Have a place within that you can retreat to, and explore your higher self. Your mental-spiritual-physical connection is not some myth that hippies and monks have created, it's a real thing that you feel. The more you connect with this the better. When you have found that balance between the three aspects of your life you will find happiness beyond your wildest dreams. There are no limits to what you are capable of when your body is running effectively with all three aspects being considered. You will notice when one area becomes neglected, because you will feel a sense of loss and look within to find what ails you. Maintaining a schedule that puts priority on your mental, spiritual, and physical well-being is the most effective way to change your life. Identify the importance of each of the three areas of your life as a whole, and what they contribute individually.

Life has become so complex as of late, and we need to take back time for ourselves, and our well-being. Everything affects everything, so if you are really taking care of yourself mentally and physically, but not spiritually, you will never find complete balance of your body. At the end of the day, we all only have so much time on the planet, and when we do pass we leave this world behind. I'm not telling you to create a relationship with God so you can go to heaven after death, I'm proposing you create a relationship with your spiritual higher self, so that you can create heaven on Earth while you embark on your journey today, right now.

Once I changed my perception in life, everything seemed to change for the better. Had things changed in an instant, or had I simply made the *choice* to be happy with what was currently in my life? It's all a choice, and one you can make this very second. Like, right now! Choose to see the good in your life, and choose to not be negatively affected by the obstacles that pop up in your life. Problems are a pretty good indicator that you are alive. Everybody has issues, but how we deal with those issues depend entirely on the person. See road blocks in your life as a test to make you absolutely stronger, or throw yourself a pity party and see if you can figure out why this only ever happens to you. I can guarantee you'll get a lot more accomplished with the go-getter attitude of option #1.

Having that positive perception also helps find the humour in situations. You need to be able to laugh at life, and especially yourself. We all make mistakes, and life sometimes really pushes you to your limits. But when you think you've reached your limit, and don't think you can take any more bad luck something even worse is going to happen, and you'll have two choices: You can either laugh about it, or cry about it.

You must develop the acceptance of the current situation, and be able to recognize whether you can truly change the circumstances or not. If you can't change it, let it go 100%. If you can change it, make a game plan and work hard to fix it. It's that simple. No more pity parties about how tough life can be. Pity parties are BS, and a total cop-out for action. Fix it, or find acceptance in it — that's the answer to all of life's problems!

One of life's problems that we struggle to correct are our relationships. We allow friends, family, and spouses to be negative influences in our lives and feel trapped to live with this negativity for the rest of our days. I hope that by now you can see that you are never stuck with anything in this life; everything is your choice. If people are treating you terribly, it is because you are allowing them to do so. Roll your eyes at me all you want, but it's just as much your fault as it is theirs. You need to make the decision of what you deserve, create clear guidelines of what they will look like to you, and begin holding your relationships accountable to your new found standards.

This new standard business is going to begin with some discomfort. You're going to be forced to communicate your new needs to your current relationship, and that will go one of three ways: They will accept it and value you enough to change their ways, they will ignore your plea and keep on doing what they have always done, or they will decide you're not worth the effort and will begin avoiding you like the plague. You must be completely comfortable with any of those outcomes before the conversations begin. Know that the people in your life that truly matter will *fit* in your life and will be a positive influence emotionally; anyone else is simply not worth having around. This doesn't need to be a negative thing. Sure it hurts, but you've got to see the big picture. When someone who is constantly bringing you down is all of a sudden out of your life (due to your decision or their own) you will open up an opportunity for a positive person to replace him or her.

That's the thing about your life, the less negativity you have in it, the more space there is for positivity to blossom. Rid yourself of volatile relationships once and for all, and truly work to find compromise on those relationships you deeply cherish. But be sure to make a list of your absolute must-haves and must-not-haves and be consistent in your relationships, and honest with yourself on which relationships are actually fulfilling your needs. Life is simply too short for negativity!

One of the most detrimental issues we can have in relationships is a lack of vulnerability, or rather lack of *comfort* with vulnerability. I was a perfect example of this in my relationship with my husband. As early as last week I caught myself making up an excuse about PMSing to explain why I was crying about something so silly. They were happy tears, but I felt ridiculous letting them go. It is a constant battle finding vulnerability acceptable and comfortable.

So many people have the idea that vulnerability is a sign of weakness, when in reality it is a sign of utmost strength and bravery. Vulnerability is showing your rawest form of self, and being genuine to your character. Many of us avoid these exposures due to our own insecurities of who we are and how much love we think we deserve. We fear that we may be rejected in this state, and that would be the worst possible reflection for who we truly are. But in reality, when we are with the people we can trust and love, they deserve nothing but our most vulnerable, true self. There is absolutely nothing more beautiful in this world than being true to yourself. When you meet someone who is genuine and totally authentic, you realize it almost immediately. It is an organic presence that is so wonderful to be around. We all have this potential, but we must make the conscious choice and effort to be ourselves.

Find your self-acceptance from within, and know that regardless of other people's perceptions or opinions, that you are absolutely perfect just the way you are. You don't need to pretend to be someone you're not, and you sure as hell don't need to omit parts of yourself in fear that people won't understand or enjoy your personality. There are and will be people who think you are absolutely fabulous and will love every single thing about you, there will also be people who don't quite fit into your style, and there is nothing wrong with that either. We can't all get along famously, and if you make that a priority, you're going to waste your life jumping through hoops to try and gain everyone's approval and admiration. The only approval that means anything to you belongs between your two ears, and that's your *own*. Love yourself, and others will love you. And the ones who don't can take a hike because you're awesome! (Just saying...)

The best way to truly grow self-love is by investing in yourself. I always say, when you begin investing in yourself, the universe begins investing in you as well. You are sending a message to the universe that you deserve good in this world, and that you are open and willing to receive abundance in all shapes and forms. This includes money, relationships, love, health, and happiness.

In order to truly love yourself, you must learn to appreciate and approve of yourself entirely. Right now. In your current state. Find acceptance that you are good enough just as your are. But in saying that, we also must make changes in the way we live our lives. We must begin to invest more into ourselves to show the universe that we are ready for a change.

Physical well-being is the perfect introduction to loving yourself and investing in yourself. Your body is the only one you get in this lifetime, and we absolutely must treat it with the utmost respect and love. Physical activity is absolutely critical in our well-being. This can be as simple as going for a daily walk, to getting a gym membership. This can be something you do on your own, or something you invite a couple of friends to join you in. Getting moving is essential to your overall health and is a surefire way to change your perspective in life. Many people I know who have started training at the gym, have begun to make other adjustments in their lives to become more consistent with their new-found health priorities. They begin to feel so good about themselves, and so great physically that they begin adjusting their diet to make the most of the efforts they are committing to daily exercise.

How can we live our lives without our health being a priority? Just like anything else we are changing, it may seem difficult at the beginning, but when you begin reaping the rewards, it becomes so incredibly exciting and you begin to create momentum in your journey. Your confidence will skyrocket, and your energy levels will soar. You will feel better than you ever have, and this will push you to commit more effort into your health and fitness.

You can't expect other people to love you, if you can't love yourself. Taking care of your physical body is one of the best ways to show yourself some love. And the list of benefits are too long to list! Commit to one diet change and one addition of any form of exercise today and see what happens in your life. You will attract so much good in your life because you have begun to invest in your own well-being. Take the time to write out some simple goals, and put some effort into your outcome each day!

Goals are such a wonderful way to not only invest into yourself, but to build your own self-confidence. There is absolutely nothing more satisfying in this world than writing down a goal, and then getting to check that goal off as complete. Especially if it was something you didn't think you could do. Goals require faith, too. They are critical for self-growth and we all know now that if you're not growing you're dying!

Make goals to cover your mental, physical and spiritual growth, and be sure to take some action as soon as you've put those goals to paper. You need to write them out to put that message out into the Universe, and to also hold yourself accountable. Never sell yourself short when it comes to goals, don't set them low so that you can easily achieve them. You must have the confidence in yourself that you can achieve anything you truly set your mind to, and shoot for the stars! You are limiting your potential significantly by limiting your hopes and dreams! Accomplishing your goals will bring a fulfillment to your life that you will never match!

Fulfillment in life is sought after by many, but rarely achieved. This is not because people have issues in their life, but rather issues with their perception of life. Fulfillment is fuelled by gratitude and gratitude can be given regardless of the situations in your life. Life is to be celebrated, in your high times, and especially during your lows. When life isn't going the way you wish it would, that is when you need to be the most grateful for what you have in your life. If you are alive, you can be grateful. Every single day six feet above ground rather than six feet under is a great day, and a day full of unlimited potential. Grasping that potential requires focus on the present moment, positivity and a clear representation of what a fulfilled life looks like to you.

Fulfillment is different for every person, so you must first declare what a perfect life looks like for you. Write down what you absolutely must-have and must-not-have to feel happy with your life, and begin directing your life in a way to make those dreams a reality. Things will not make you happy if you are not happy with yourself. If you haven't the faintest idea how to love yourself completely, you will never find true happiness. If you do not love yourself, you will never truly believe you deserve good in this life, and thus you will always sabotage yourself from having everything you've ever dreamt of.

When you love yourself, your life is fulfilled. You will find happiness in every situation life throws at you, and you will not need the love of others to validate your existence. You will validate yourself, continuously, and will be so filled with love that people will naturally be attracted to you anyways. You will have people lined up to be a part of this wonderful life you have created, because when you feel good about yourself, you make others feel good too. And you begin to intrigue others to follow in your path to self-fulfillment. This personal enlightenment costs you nothing, but pays out in dividends you couldn't possibly imagine.

Don't wait until the circumstances in your life change to feel fulfilled, make the decision right now, in this moment, to feel fulfilled with what you currently have. Appreciate the air that you breathe, and the luxuries we take advantage of every single day. Be thankful for the amazing people in your life, and the job that you have. Be thankful for the inconveniences too, because they help transform you into a stronger, more patient person. The hardships in our lives make us more resilient, and without them we will never grow. We must find fulfillment in our challenges as much as our victories, for they all add a zest to our life. A life without struggle would be meaningless and boring. See adversity as a test of your character, and try to ace it. And if you fail miserably, well study the materials you were given so that the next time you are more prepared. Every lesson simply adds to your education, and if that lesson cost you a lot of money, try to remember that education generally *is* an expensive process. Consider yourself a graduate of life, and you've just completed your Masters in what not to do. Print yourself out a little certificate and frame in on the wall if you feel it's appropriate. I would personally run out of wall space to hang my certificates if I followed through on this suggestion!

Life is a beautiful, wonderful, messy experience and it is special for each and every one of us. You can live the life of your dreams right now, in this very moment, just as I have. I am wrapping up this book, without any promise of its success, and yet I am fulfilled beyond a shadow of a doubt, because I know that I am following my dreams. One step at a time, I am following my destiny.

This journey is what makes life magical.

This journey gives me a purpose.

This journey is a complete success, regardless of the outcome, because I set a goal and put everything I had into it.

We only get one opportunity to live this life, and my hope is that you will connect with yourself on a level you've never reached before, dig deep and find that love for yourself, and then go live your life with every ounce of passion and enthusiasm you can muster. Because true happiness and fulfillment is achievable, you simply need to make the decision to embrace it. That's the secret to life!

Know that my heart and soul are with you along your journey, and I feel so blessed to have had the opportunity to be a part of it. I truly hope that I have served you in some way.

All my love,
LK Elliott

Epilogue: Life After Confessions

It has been a year since I wrote *Confessions of an Ex Hot Mess*, and I have had an incredible year of growth. It has been a year full of ups and downs. After writing the book and reading it over and over again, I was reminded of all the gems I have learned along my journey. This reminder caused me to make some drastic changes in my life, and that has resulted in opportunities and fulfillment that exceeded my wildest expectations.

Let's begin by mentioning sacrifice, because this has played a critical role in many of the successes I have achieved lately. I made the conscious decision to give up many old habits that were no longer serving me and my destiny. I mentioned earlier that I had adopted a vegetarian lifestyle, and that is still something I am practising. I feel stronger physically than ever and absolutely love everything about this lifestyle. But what good is a diet change if I am continuing to poison myself with alcohol?

For me, alcohol was not only a poison that caused physical pain and sickness, but it was a cancer in my relationships. I let down friends, family, my husband, and most importantly myself when I was drinking. This habit had to go. The longer I went without, the less I yearned for the experience of drinking. I began to see alcohol for what it was. I began to recognize that the act of "celebrating" with food and alcohol was simply a marketing scheme created by the food and alcohol industry to increase their profits. I celebrate in much healthier ways now!

As soon as I gave up drinking, I gave up the excuse of "I only did that because I was drunk". I became instantly responsible for every one of my actions, which was much easier to do when my inhibitions weren't being compromised by alcoholic influence. I also became much more productive, by avoiding the much dreaded hangover after a night of over indulgence. I had less to apologize for. I had more control over the outcome of my life. I had much better relationships.

My marriage has never been stronger either. My husband and I both took the same stance the day after our honeymoon. We agreed it was time to get serious about our lives and our goals, and that we must sacrifice simple pleasures like drinking for the potential of a much better life. And that is exactly what that decision has brought to us: the life of our wildest dreams. We want to change the world for the better, and I know with the amount of work that we have been investing into our dreams, that the outcome is sure to come eventually, probably sooner than later.

I have also sacrificed a lot of my "downtime" with friends and family. This is a sacrifice I have been willing to make, but has been very hard for those around me to understand. You see, you become your five closest friends, so if your friends are living lives that do not reflect what you want for yourself, you need to find new friends. I know this sounds harsh, but I hear this time and time again from incredibly successful people in all industries from fitness to finance. From people I respect, admire and aspire to be like.

It's like playing tennis for example: If you only play against people who are less talented than you, you are never going to become a better tennis player. It is only when you play against people who are stronger than you, that you are forced to grow and improve in order to compete and be successful.

While you are hanging out with friends, partying, and playing around there is always someone out there who is working hard towards their goals. There is always someone who is taking that same amount of time and using it to become a better version of themselves. For me, I have made the decision to be that person who is working harder. That is not to say I do not allow myself time to enjoy life, I do, but only if I have earned it. Relaxation and rest must be earned in my life. This new found work ethic has brought opportunities to me that I couldn't have even imagined a year ago.

In the past year I have competed in my first ever fitness competition, enjoyed my first photo-shoot, been featured in my first fitness magazine, been contacted by a modelling agency, and am in the process of having my first book published. None of these things could have happened without the sacrifice and hard work I have invested into my life. I haven't waited around for things to happen, I have worked so hard that results were inevitable. I feel really great about what I have accomplished so far, and am looking forward to seeing what the future has in store for me.

Confessions of an Ex Hot Mess has taught me so much about myself, and has helped me improve the quality of my own life dramatically. It has given me strength from within that I never knew I had. It has helped me conquer my own fears that have limited my success up until this point, and has helped me push through one of the biggest losses of my life: the death of my grandfather.

Five days before my first ever photo-shoot (with a prestigious fitness photographer) I received one of the most devastating phone calls of my life. My grandfather had been admitted into the hospital a week prior to have surgery, and after a few days of recovery he was released from the hospital and sent home. I was relieved to hear about how great he was feeling and was looking forward to visiting in a month's time and to tell him all about my modelling adventure which was soon upon me. A mere three hours after a progress text from my Dad telling me how great my "Papa" was doing, I received a phone call stating he had suffered a fatal stroke and was gone.

I felt like the floor had fallen down from beneath me. I was in shock and horror.

To make matters worse, I had to decide the fate of a trip across the country for my photo-shoot, which I truly felt was going to change my life forever. I was heartbroken and didn't know how I could possibly move on from such heartache. But even in a state of despair I was able to ground myself and find a way to move forward. I made the decision that the last thing my Papa would have wanted was for me to miss out on this opportunity, and my grandmother agreed. She offered to postpone the funeral so that I could pursue my dreams. I understood that this photo-shoot was now much more than a day to capture images, it was so much more than I had originally intended. I needed to dig deeper than ever before and continue my strenuous fitness regime to maintain a look worthy of the opportunity. As a result, I didn't miss a single workout. I didn't eat a single food outside of my diet. I woke up the next morning with a fire burning within brighter than ever. I had to do this to honour my Papa. I had to live my life with more passion than ever to honour the life he had lost.

Rather than choosing grief, I chose motivation. My Papa had taught me in that moment that life is not to be taken for granted. Life is short, and I could not afford to waste a single day crying over what I had lost, when I could be fighting harder for what I desired. And that is exactly what I did. I rocked the photo-shoot and impressed my photographer. I then fully enjoyed every day I spent on vacation with my husband, because I had a renewed appreciation for the simple gift of life.

My faith in life and the universe helped me cope with the loss of my Papa, and I feel him here with me even after his passing. I see a great contrast between this loss and the loss of my first grandfather five years ago. Seeing how I was able to find strength from within, push through the pain, and achieve success despite adversity shows me how far I have come emotionally and mentally. I have filled my life with a better support system, and most importantly I have created a stronger foundation within that allows me to maintain stability even when the going gets tough. This is something I have developed since writing my *Confessions* and it is a gift that I hope to be able to pass on to other readers as well.

After the photo-shoot, I came home to reflect on such an eventful couple of weeks. I had learned so much about myself, and how strong I could be. You truly have no idea how strong you are until being strong is the only option you have. Conquering a road block of that intensity made me question every fear I had ever had. I realized that the life of my dreams truly was being sabotaged by my fear of failure. I came home a new woman. I had become a woman who refused to accept fear into her life. I was determined to chase my dreams unapologetically, and without concerns of judgment, criticism or a lack of approval from those around me. I didn't need their approval to live the life of my dreams. They can apply their own rules to their own lives, and I will apply my rules to mine.

This was a great lesson to me. Just because someone else has a rule, does not make it a rule for you. If someone has a limitation in their life, that does not mean it is a limitation in yours. I became aware of the fact that the Universe wants me to achieve my wildest dreams and live life with fulfillment, but I was putting up road blocks of my own to ensure I never reached my destination.

I now make the decision to open my heart to the possibilities of my own potential, and to start working towards my dreams with a complete surrender of the outcome. I will focus on working my a★★

off while I allow the Universe to work out the details of my fate. I have faith that my dreams will come true if my intentions are pure and my work ethic is relentless.

Within two days of being home from my trip I had received a phone call from a photographer who wanted to do a stylized shoot with me, a modelling agency who wanted to represent me, and a publishing company who wanted to help get my book published. These opportunities had always been there, but I wasn't willing to let them in. It wasn't until I opened my heart and freed myself from limiting beliefs and fears that the true potential of my life could appear. This is the power of love, positivity, and the law of attraction.

Today I am being blissfully bombarded with modelling opportunities, which I have found a great passion in. I have created wonderful habits to keep my body in the best shape of its life. My marriage is growing stronger every single day. My book is soon to be published. And I know with all certainty that this is just the beginning.

Dreams do come true, but you must allow them to realize.

I knew my 27th year of life would be spectacular because 27 has always been my lucky number, but I am delighted to report that I no longer feel the need to rely on luck for my success. I realize that success has everything to do with your mindset, your faith, your work ethic and your passion for whatever it is you are dreaming about. Success is as simple as picking something you absolutely cannot live without, and making small strides every single day to bring you closer to obtaining that goal. Never settle in life, and don't waste time dreaming small. If the Universe wants you to be successful, why would you limit yourself to small, achievable dreams when you could be doing something extraordinary?

The fishing is best where the fewest go and the collective insecurity of the world makes it easy for people to hit home runs while everyone is aiming for base hits.

-Timothy Ferriss

Writing this book has taught me more than I ever imagined, and my dream is that these lessons will be inherited by each reader who takes the time to open these pages. Daily I take the time to visualize myself at book signings, meeting readers who tell me this book has helped them in some way. That is my dream. It's not about making money, it's about making a difference. I like to think about what my obituary might read one day. I don't need it to say that I was the wealthiest author to have ever lived (although I won't object if the Universe insists!) I need it to say that I positively impacted the lives of people I came in contact with, through personal interaction or simply through the words I have written. Take a moment and ask yourself, what do you want your obituary to say? What do you want to be remembered by? What will be your legacy?

Then take a look at your life today, and recognize the differences between that obituary and what you are accomplishing right now. Recognize the differences and make some changes. Change your expectations for life and open your heart to the full range of opportunities and potential within yourself. Think like a child on Christmas Eve: they don't want one little gift, they want everything and anything they can get their hands on. Why can't we think like that sometimes? Why do we put limits on our life? Why do we put limits on our dreams?

Be everything you ever dreamt of being. And be that person today, not tomorrow.

It doesn't matter who you were yesterday, or even an hour ago. This moment is the only one you have control over, so make the most of it. Seize this day in honour of everyone who couldn't be here today to do the same. Seize this day to honour yourself. Seize this day because you have everything you need within you to make your dreams a reality.

You deserve everything this world has to offer. You deserve happiness and fulfillment.

Everything you have ever dreamt of is on the other side of that door, and all you need to do is open it up and receive. Open your heart, mind, and spirit and allow your life to change for the better. Breathe in the positive, and exhale the negative. It's as simple as that.

A man is not made wise by knowing everything there is to know, he is wise because he realizes he will never know everything there is to know. Continue on your journey of growth, and never stop seeking more resources to help you along your path. Ask questions to those who have what you want. Ask yourself what you can do everyday to get closer to your goals and dreams.

I have listed a few great resources below to consider adding to your collection, as I have found great wisdom and strength within them. Live with passion my friends.

Hot Mess Healing Must Haves:

Feeling Good Handbook by Dr. David Burns

Get the Edge Audio by Anthony Robbins

Why You're Not Married... Yet by Tracy McMillan

You Can Heal Your Life by Louise Hay

Esteem Affirmations Audio by Louise Hay

Online References:

Change Your Thoughts, Change Your World: Jennifer Read Hawthorn (www.jenniferhawthorne.com/articles/change_your_thoughts.html)

3 Myths about Vulnerability: Margarita Tartakovsky, M.S (http://psychcentral.com/blog/ archives/2012/08/29/3-myths-about -vulnerability/#.UrySybSUoy4)

Ready for a Vulnerability Hangover? Five ideas from Brené Brown: Roman Krznaric (http://www.romankrznaric.com/outrospection/2012/10/16/1729)

The 12 Cognitive Biases That Prevent You From Being Rational: George Dvorsky (http:// io9.com/5974468/the-most-common-cognitive-biases-that-prevent-you from-being-rational)

CPSIA information can be obtained
at www.ICGtesting.com
Printed in the USA
BVOW08s2010130917
494776BV00002B/254/P

9 781460 258262